low-fat

HOMESTYLE

low-fat

bay books

contents

Eating healthy with low-fat

Let's face it—fat makes food taste great. There's nothing quite like the intense satisfaction that butter, oil, cream, various cheeses and other rich foods can provide … but there are also potentially disastrous health consequences if we indulge in them too enthusiastically. Most of us could do well to consume less fat but, it has to be said, even the very thought of trimming some of that yummy fat from our diets can seem like a monumental bore. It's more than a little unfair that the foods that arguably taste the best are among the worst for our wellbeing, not to mention our waistlines.

Adopting a low-fat approach to eating doesn't necessarily mean being consigned to a regimen of dreary, thin-flavoured 'rabbit' food. We can still have our carrot cake (and our couscous, curry and chicken chasseur) and eat it too! With *Homestyle Low-fat*, you'll discover a world of foods and flavours so diverse and so delicious that not for a single moment will you feel as though you are 'missing out'. After all, how good do slow-cooked lamb shanks, seafood ravioli soup, smoked salmon pizzas and creamy rice pots sound?

Of course, we've all realised ages ago that salads, vegetable soups, fish, grilled lean meats, tomato-laden pasta sauces and puddings based on fruits are lower in the fat stakes than most other dishes. And all these usual suspects are well-represented here, with the scrumptious likes of curried sweet potato soup, lime and prawn salad, Asian barbecued chicken, pasta pomodoro, and berries in Champagne jelly. But the really exciting thing about this book is that all those favourite, comforting friends—namely, the dishes you thought you'd have to completely give up, forever—are collected here too. They are slightly trimmed down, but not so much that you'd really notice: moussaka, spaghetti bolognese, beef pot roast, lasagne, lamb casserole with beans, and coq au vin. There are even recipes for lemon berry cheesecake, fudge brownies and tiramisu! Low-fat cooking (and, more importantly, low-fat eating) has never sounded, nor tasted, as absolutely fabulous as it does in these pages. So now there's really no excuse left, is there?

Soups and starters

Potato, broccoli and coriander soup

PREPARATION TIME: 15 MINUTES | TOTAL COOKING TIME: 30 MINUTES | SERVES 6

500 g (1 lb 2 oz) broccoli
cooking oil spray
2 onions, finely chopped
2 garlic cloves, finely chopped
2 teaspoons ground cumin
1 teaspoon ground coriander
750 g (1 lb 10 oz) potatoes, cubed
2 small chicken stock (bouillon) cubes
375 ml (13 fl oz/1½ cups) skim milk
3 tablespoons finely chopped coriander (cilantro)

NUTRITION PER SERVE
Protein 10 g; Fat 0.5 g; Carbohydrate 20 g; Dietary Fibre 6 g; Cholesterol 2 mg; 580 kJ (140 Cal)

1 Cut the broccoli into small pieces. Lightly spray the base of a large saucepan with oil, then place over medium heat and add the onion and garlic. Add 1 tablespoon water to prevent sticking. Cover and cook, stirring occasionally, over low heat for 5 minutes, or until the onion has softened and is lightly golden. Add the ground cumin and coriander and cook for 2 minutes.

2 Add the potato and broccoli to the pan, stir well and add the stock cubes and 1 litre (35 fl oz/4 cups) water. Slowly bring to the boil, reduce the heat, cover and simmer over low heat for 20 minutes, or until the vegetables are tender. Allow to cool slightly.

3 Blend the soup in batches in a food processor or blender until smooth. Return to the pan and stir in the milk. Slowly reheat, without boiling. Stir the chopped coriander through and season well before serving.

Chop all the broccoli into small, even-sized florets for quick cooking.

Stir the ground cumin and coriander into the onion and cook for about 2 minutes.

Purée the mixture in batches, in a food processor or blender, until it is smooth.

Won ton noodle soup

PREPARATION TIME: 25 MINUTES | TOTAL COOKING TIME: 25 MINUTES | SERVES 4

70 g (2½ oz) raw prawns (shrimp)
70 g (2½ oz) minced (ground) veal
3 tablespoons soy sauce
1 tablespoon finely chopped spring onion (scallion)
1 tablespoon finely chopped water chestnuts
1 teaspoon finely chopped fresh ginger
2 garlic cloves, finely chopped
24 gow gee wrappers
1.25 litres (44 fl oz/5 cups) chicken stock
2 tablespoons mirin
500 g (1 lb 2 oz) baby bok choy (pak choy), finely shredded
8 spring onions (scallions), sliced

1 Peel, devein and finely chop the prawns. Mix with the minced veal, 2 teaspoons soy sauce, spring onion, water chestnuts, ginger and garlic. Lay the round wrappers out on a work surface and place a teaspoon of mixture in the middle of each.

2 Moisten the edges of the wrappers and bring up the sides to form a pouch. Pinch together to seal. Cook in batches in a large saucepan of rapidly boiling water for 4–5 minutes. Drain and divide among soup bowls.

3 Bring the stock, remaining soy sauce and mirin to the boil in a large saucepan. Add the bok choy, cover and simmer for 2 minutes, or until the bok choy has just wilted. Add the sliced spring onion and season. Ladle the stock, bok choy and spring onion over the won tons.

Peel the prawns and devein them before chopping them finely.

Bring the sides of the wrappers up around the filling and pinch to seal.

NUTRITION PER SERVE
Protein 10 g; Fat 5 g; Carbohydrate 30 g; Dietary Fibre 5 g; Cholesterol 25 mg; 760 kJ (180 Cal)

Chicken noodle and mushroom soup

PREPARATION TIME: 10 MINUTES | TOTAL COOKING TIME: 10 MINUTES | SERVES 6

cooking oil spray
2 teaspoons grated fresh ginger
4 spring onions (scallions), finely chopped
1 boneless, skinless chicken breast, cut into thin strips
120 g (4¼ oz) button mushrooms, sliced
410 g (14½ oz) tin chicken consommé
60 g (2¼ oz) instant noodles
3 teaspoons kecap manis (see NOTE)

1 Heat a little oil in a saucepan, add the ginger, spring onion and chicken and stir-fry over high heat for 4–5 minutes, or until the chicken changes colour. Add the mushrooms and cook for a further 1 minute.

2 Add the consommé and 500 ml (17 fl oz/ 2 cups) water and bring to the boil. Stir in the noodles, then reduce the heat and simmer for 3 minutes, or until the noodles are soft. Stir in the kecap manis and serve.

NOTE: *Kecap manis is a thick, sweet soy sauce available from Asian grocery stores. If you cannot find it, use regular soy sauce with a little soft brown sugar added, as a substitute.*

Stir-fry the ginger, spring onion and chicken over high heat for 5 minutes.

Add the consommé and water, then add the noodles and cook until soft.

NUTRITION PER SERVE
Protein 9 g; Fat 6.5 g; Carbohydrate 4 g; Dietary Fibre 1 g; Cholesterol 20 mg; 520 kJ (110 Cal)

capel vale
Debut
2007
verdelho

Seafood ravioli in gingery soup

PREPARATION TIME: 30 MINUTES | TOTAL COOKING TIME: 20 MINUTES | SERVES 4

8 raw prawns (shrimp), about 250 g (9 oz)
1 carrot, chopped
1 onion, chopped
1 celery stalk, chopped
3 spring onions (scallions), thinly sliced
6 cm (2½ inch) piece fresh ginger, thinly shredded
1 tablespoon mirin
1 teaspoon kecap manis (see NOTE, page 13)
1 tablespoon soy sauce
4 large scallops
100 g (3½ oz) boneless white fish fillet
1 egg white
200 g (7 oz) gow gee wrappers
1 medium handful coriander (cilantro) leaves

NUTRITION PER SERVE
Protein 17 g; Fat 7 g; Carbohydrate 65 g; Dietary Fibre 4.5 g; Cholesterol 125 mg; 1765 kJ (420 Cal)

1 To make the soup, peel and devein the prawns, reserve four for the ravioli filling and chop the rest into small pieces and reserve. Put the prawn heads and shells in a large frying pan, cook over high heat until starting to brown, then cover with 1 litre (35 fl oz/4 cups) water. Add the carrot, onion and celery, bring to the boil, reduce the heat and simmer for 10 minutes. Strain and discard the prawn heads, shells and vegetables. Return the stock to a clean pan and add the spring onion, ginger, mirin, kecap manis and soy sauce. Set aside.

2 To make the ravioli, chop the whole reserved prawns with the scallops and fish in a food processor until smooth. Add enough egg white to bind. Lay half the round wrappers on a work surface and place a rounded teaspoon of filling in the centre of each. Brush the edges with water. Top each with another wrapper and press the edges to seal, eliminating air bubbles as you go. Trim with a fluted cutter. Cover with plastic wrap.

3 Bring a large saucepan of water to the boil. Meanwhile, heat the stock and leave simmering. Just prior to serving, drop a few ravioli at a time into the boiling water. Cook for 2 minutes, remove with a slotted spoon and divide among heated bowls. Cook the chopped reserved prawns in the same water for 2 minutes; drain. Pour the hot stock over the ravioli and serve, sprinkled with the chopped cooked prawns and coriander leaves.

Stir the prawn heads and shells in a pan over high heat until lightly browned.

Brush the edge of one wrapper with water, then cover with another.

Cook each batch of ravioli for 2 minutes, then remove with a slotted spoon.

Curried sweet potato soup

PREPARATION TIME: 20 MINUTES | TOTAL COOKING TIME: 40 MINUTES | SERVES 6

1 tablespoon oil
1 large onion, chopped
2 garlic cloves, crushed
3 teaspoons curry powder
1.25 kg (2 lb 12 oz) orange sweet potato, peeled and cubed
1 litre (35 fl oz/4 cups) chicken stock
1 large apple, peeled, cored and grated
125 ml (4 fl oz/½ cup) light coconut milk

1 Heat the oil in a large saucepan over medium heat and cook the onion for 10 minutes, stirring occasionally, until very soft. Add the garlic and curry powder and cook for a further 1 minute.

2 Add the sweet potato, stock and apple. Bring to the boil, reduce the heat and simmer, partially covered, for 30 minutes, until very soft.

3 Cool the soup a little before processing in batches until smooth. Return to the pan, stir in the coconut milk and reheat gently without boiling. Serve with warm pitta bread.

STORAGE TIME: *Can be kept in the fridge for 1 day without the coconut milk: add this when you reheat.*

NUTRITION PER SERVE
Protein 5 g; Fat 8 g; Carbohydrate 35 g; Dietary Fibre 5.5 g; Cholesterol 0 mg; 975 kJ (233 Cal)

Add the garlic and curry powder to the softened onion and cook for another minute.

Stir in the stock with the cubed sweet potato and grated apple.

Once the soup has been processed stir in the coconut milk.

Minestrone

PREPARATION TIME: 30 MINUTES + OVERNIGHT SOAKING | TOTAL COOKING TIME: 2¾ HOURS | SERVES 8

250 g (9 oz) dried borlotti beans
2 tablespoons olive oil
2 onions, chopped
2 garlic cloves, crushed
90 g (3¼ oz) bacon slices, chopped
4 roma (plum) tomatoes, peeled and chopped
3 tablespoons chopped parsley
2 litres (70 fl oz/8 cups) beef or vegetable stock
3 tablespoons red wine
1 carrot, chopped
1 swede (rutabaga), peeled and diced
2 potatoes, cubed
3 tablespoons tomato paste (concentrated purée)
2 zucchini (courgettes), sliced
90 g (3¼ oz) peas
90 g (3¼ oz) small macaroni
parmesan cheese, to serve

1 Soak the borlotti beans in water overnight then drain. Add to a saucepan of boiling water, simmer for 15 minutes and then drain. Heat the oil in a large heavy-based pan and cook the onion, garlic and bacon pieces until the onion is soft and the bacon golden.

2 Add the tomato, parsley, borlotti beans, stock and red wine. Simmer, covered, over low heat for 2 hours. Add the carrot, swede, potato and tomato paste, cover and simmer for a further 15–20 minutes.

3 Add the zucchini, peas and pasta. Cover and simmer for 10–15 minutes, or until the vegetables and macaroni are tender. Season and serve with a little grated parmesan.

VARIATION: *For a lighter taste, use chicken stock instead of the beef stock and omit the bacon.*

NUTRITION PER SERVE
Protein 15 g; Fat 7 g; Carbohydrate 25 g; Dietary Fibre 10 g; Cholesterol 12 mg; 955 kJ (228 Cal)

Soak the borlotti beans in a bowl of water overnight and then drain.

Use a sharp knife to peel and dice the swede and other vegetables.

Tom yam goong

PREPARATION TIME: 25 MINUTES | TOTAL COOKING TIME: 45 MINUTES | SERVES 6

500 g (1 lb 2 oz) raw prawns (shrimp)
1 tablespoon oil
2 tablespoons tom yam curry paste
2 tablespoons tamarind purée
2 teaspoons ground turmeric
1 teaspoon chopped small red chillies
4 makrut (kaffir lime) leaves, shredded, plus extra, to garnish
2 tablespoons fish sauce
2 tablespoons lime juice
2 teaspoons grated palm sugar (jaggery) or soft brown sugar

NUTRITION PER SERVE
Protein 15 g; Fat 5 g; Carbohydrate 11 g; Dietary Fibre 1.3 g; Cholesterol 158 mg; 608 kJ (145 Cal)

1 Peel the prawns, leaving the tails intact. Devein the prawns, starting at the head end. Reserve the shells and heads. Cover and refrigerate the prawn meat. Heat the oil in a wok or large saucepan and cook the shells and heads over medium heat, stirring frequently, for 10 minutes, or until the shells turn orange.

2 Add 250 ml (9 fl oz/1 cup) water and the tom yam paste to the pan. Bring to the boil and cook for 5 minutes, or until reduced slightly. Add another 2 litres (70 fl oz/8 cups) water, bring to the boil, reduce the heat and simmer for 20 minutes. Strain, discarding the shells and heads, and return the stock to the pan.

3 Add the tamarind purée, turmeric, chilli and makrut leaves to the pan, bring to the boil and cook for 2 minutes. Add the prawn meat and cook for 5 minutes, or until pink. Stir in the fish sauce, lime juice and sugar. Garnish with shredded makrut leaves.

Makrut leaves can be tough and need to be very finely shredded before use.

Cook the prawn shells and tom yam paste until the liquid has reduced and thickened slightly.

Stir in the tamarind purée, turmeric, chilli and makrut leaves and cook for 2 minutes.

Roasted red capsicum soup

PREPARATION TIME: 50 MINUTES | TOTAL COOKING TIME: 1 HOUR | SERVES 6

4 large red capsicums (peppers)
4 ripe tomatoes
2 tablespoons oil
1 red onion, chopped
1 garlic clove, crushed
1 litre (35 fl oz/4 cups) vegetable stock
1 teaspoon sweet chilli sauce
parmesan cheese and pesto, to serve (optional)

1 Cut the capsicums into large flat pieces, removing the seeds and membrane. Place skin side up under a hot grill (broiler) until blackened. Leave covered with a tea towel (dish towel) until cool, then peel away the skin and chop the flesh.

2 Score a small cross in the base of each tomato, put them in a large heatproof bowl and cover with boiling water. Leave for 1 minute, then plunge into cold water and peel the skin from the cross. Cut in half, scoop out the seeds and roughly chop the flesh.

3 Heat the oil in a large heavy-based saucepan and add the onion. Cook over medium heat for 10 minutes, stirring frequently, until very soft. Add the garlic and cook for a further 1 minute. Add the capsicum, tomato and stock; bring to the boil, reduce the heat and simmer for about 20 minutes.

4 Purée the soup in a food processor or blender until smooth (in batches if necessary). Return to the pan to reheat gently and stir in the chilli sauce. Serve topped with shavings of parmesan and a little pesto, if desired.

Once the skin of the capsicum has been blackened it should peel away easily.

Scoring a cross in the base of the tomato makes it easier to remove the skin.

NUTRITION PER SERVE
Protein 3 g; Fat 7 g; Carbohydrate 5 g; Dietary Fibre 2 g; Cholesterol 0 mg; 380 kJ (90 Cal)

Thai chicken balls

PREPARATION TIME: 20 MINUTES | TOTAL COOKING TIME: 40 MINUTES | SERVES 6

1 kg (2 lb 4 oz) minced (ground) chicken
90 g (3¼ oz/1 cup) fresh breadcrumbs
4 spring onions (scallions), sliced
1 tablespoon ground coriander
3 very large handfuls coriander (cilantro), chopped, plus extra leaves, to garnish
3 tablespoons sweet chilli sauce
1–2 tablespoons lemon juice
2 tablespoons oil
quartered lime, to serve

1 Preheat the oven to 200°C (400°F/Gas 6). Mix the minced chicken and breadcrumbs in a large bowl.

2 Add the spring onion, ground and fresh coriander, chilli sauce and lemon juice, and mix well. Using damp hands, form the mixture into evenly shaped smaller balls or larger burger patties.

3 Heat the oil in a large non-stick frying pan and cook the chicken balls over high heat until browned all over. Drain well on paper towels and then place them on a baking tray and bake (5 minutes for balls or 10–15 minutes for patties), until cooked through. Serve with lime quarters and garnish with coriander leaves.

NUTRITION PER SERVE
Protein 40 g; Fat 8 g; Carbohydrate 10 g; Dietary Fibre 1 g; Cholesterol 85 mg; 1160 kJ (275 Cal)

Mix the spring onion, coriander, chilli sauce and lemon juice into the mince mixture.

With damp hands, form the mixture into evenly shaped balls.

Fry the chicken balls in batches until they are browned and then bake in the oven.

Chargrilled vegetable terrine

PREPARATION TIME: 30 MINUTES + OVERNIGHT REFRIGERATION | TOTAL COOKING TIME: NIL | SERVES 8

350 g (12 oz) ricotta cheese
2 garlic cloves, crushed
8 large slices chargrilled eggplant (aubergine), drained (see NOTE)
10 slices chargrilled red capsicum (pepper), drained
8 slices chargrilled zucchini (courgette), drained
100 g (3½ oz) marinated mushrooms, drained and halved
45 g (1½ oz) rocket (arugula) leaves
3 marinated artichokes, drained and sliced
85 g (3 oz) semi-dried (sun-blushed) tomatoes, drained and chopped

NUTRITION PER SERVE
Protein 6 g; Fat 5 g; Carbohydrate 3 g; Dietary Fibre 2 g; Cholesterol 20 mg; 350 kJ (85 Cal)

1 Line a 24 x 13 x 6 cm (9½ x 5 x 2½ inch) loaf tin with plastic wrap, leaving a generous amount hanging over the sides. Place the ricotta and garlic in a bowl and beat until smooth. Season with salt and pepper to taste and set aside.

2 Line the base of the tin with half the eggplant, cutting and fitting to cover the base. Top with a layer of half the capsicum, then all the zucchini slices. Spread evenly with the ricotta mixture and press down firmly. Top with a layer of half the mushrooms. Place the rocket leaves on top of the mushrooms. Arrange the artichoke, tomato and remaining mushrooms in three rows lengthways on top of the rocket.

3 Top with another layer of capsicum and finish with the eggplant. Fold the overhanging plastic wrap over the top of the terrine. Put a piece of cardboard on top and weigh it down with weights or small food tins. Refrigerate the terrine overnight.

4 To serve, peel back the plastic wrap and turn the terrine out onto a plate. Remove the plastic wrap and cut the terrine into thick slices.

NOTE: *You can buy chargrilled eggplant, capsicum and zucchini, and marinated mushrooms and artichokes at delicatessens.*

STORAGE TIME: *Cover any leftovers with plastic wrap and store in the refrigerator for up to 2 days.*

Put the ricotta and crushed garlic in a bowl and beat until smooth.

Arrange the artichoke, tomato and mushrooms in three rows over the rocket.

Cover the terrine with cardboard and weigh down with small food tins.

Soy chicken wings

PREPARATION TIME: 10 MINUTES + 20 MINUTES REFRIGERATION | TOTAL COOKING TIME: 50 MINUTES | SERVES 4

125 ml (4 fl oz/½ cup) soy sauce
3 tablespoons honey
2 garlic cloves, crushed
3 tablespoons sweet chilli sauce
4 tablespoons lemon juice
1 very large handful mint, roughly chopped
16 chicken wings

1 Preheat the oven to 200°C (400°F/Gas 6). Mix together the soy sauce, honey, garlic, sweet chilli sauce, lemon juice and mint. Put the chicken wings in a flat dish in a single layer, pour the marinade over the top, cover with plastic wrap and refrigerate for 20 minutes.

2 Place the wings and marinade into a baking dish and bake for 50 minutes, or until the wings are cooked through and the soy marinade has caramelised. Turn the wings once or twice during cooking to ensure even caramelisation.

NOTE: *The wings can be eaten by themselves or, for a main course, serve with steamed rice and a green salad. They can be marinated overnight and cooked the next day.*

Arrange the chicken wings in a single layer in a dish and pour the marinade over the top.

Bake for 50 minutes, or until the soy marinade has caramelised.

NUTRITION PER SERVE
Protein 25 g; Fat 7 g; Carbohydrate 18 g; Dietary Fibre 0 g; Cholesterol 105 mg; 1004 kJ (240 Cal)

Prawn nori rolls

PREPARATION TIME: 15 MINUTES + 1 HOUR REFRIGERATION | TOTAL COOKING TIME: 5 MINUTES | MAKES 25 ROLLS

500 g (1 lb 2 oz) raw prawns (shrimp), peeled and deveined
1½ tablespoons fish sauce
1 tablespoon sake
2 tablespoons chopped coriander (cilantro)
1 large fresh makrut (kaffir lime) leaf, finely shredded
1 tablespoon lime juice
2 teaspoons sweet chilli sauce
1 egg white, lightly beaten
5 sheets nori (dried seaweed)

DIPPING SAUCE

3 tablespoons sake
3 tablespoons soy sauce
1 tablespoon mirin
1 tablespoon lime juice

1 Process the prawns in a food processor or blender with the fish sauce, sake, coriander, makrut leaf, lime juice and sweet chilli sauce, until smooth. Add the egg white and pulse for a few seconds to just combine.

2 Lay the nori sheets on a flat surface and spread some prawn mixture over each sheet, leaving a 2 cm (¾ inch) border at one end. Roll up tightly, cover and refrigerate for 1 hour to firm. Using a sharp knife, trim the ends and cut into 2 cm (¾ inch) lengths.

3 Place the rolls in a lined bamboo steamer. Cover the steamer and place it over a wok of simmering water, making sure it doesn't touch the water. Steam the rolls for about 5 minutes.

4 For the dipping sauce, thoroughly mix all the ingredients together in a small bowl. Serve with the nori rolls.

Spread prawn mixture over each nori sheet, leaving a 2 cm (¾ inch) border at one end.

Roll each sheet up tightly, then cover and refrigerate to firm.

NUTRITION PER ROLL
Protein 4 g; Fat 0.5 g; Carbohydrate 0.5 g; Dietary Fibre 0.5 g; Cholesterol 39.5 mg; 95 kJ (23 Cal)

Chargrilled baby octopus

PREPARATION TIME: 15 MINUTES + OVERNIGHT MARINATING | TOTAL COOKING TIME: 10 MINUTES | SERVES 4

1 kg (2 lb 4 oz) baby octopus
185 ml (6 fl oz/¾ cup) red wine
2 tablespoons balsamic vinegar
2 tablespoons soy sauce
2 tablespoons hoisin sauce
1 garlic clove, crushed
cooking oil spray

NUTRITION PER SERVE
Protein 42.5 g; Fat 3.5 g; Carbohydrate 4 g; Dietary Fibre 1 g; Cholesterol 497.5 mg; 1060 kJ (255 Cal)

1 Cut off the octopus heads below the eyes with a sharp knife. Discard the heads and guts. Push the beaks out with your index finger, remove and discard. Wash the octopus thoroughly under running water and drain on crumpled paper towels. If the octopus are large, cut the tentacles into quarters.

2 Put the octopus in a large bowl. Stir together the wine, vinegar, soy sauce, hoisin sauce and garlic in a bowl and pour over the octopus. Toss to coat, then cover and refrigerate for several hours, or overnight.

3 Heat a chargrill pan or barbecue grill plate or flat plate until very hot and then lightly oil. Drain the octopus, reserving the marinade. Cook in batches for 3–5 minutes, or until the octopus flesh turns white. Brush the marinade over the octopus during cooking. Be careful not to overcook or the octopus will be tough. Serve warm or cold. Delicious with a green salad and lime wedges.

Remove and discard the head from each octopus with a sharp knife.

Push the beaks out through the centre with your index finger.

Brush the octopus all over with the reserved marinade while cooking.

Salads

Tofu salad with ginger miso dressing

PREPARATION TIME: 20 MINUTES + OVERNIGHT MARINATING | TOTAL COOKING TIME: 5 MINUTES | SERVES 4

90 ml (3 fl oz) light soy sauce
2 teaspoons soy bean oil
2 garlic cloves, crushed
1 teaspoon grated fresh ginger
1 teaspoon chilli paste
500 g (1 lb 2 oz) firm tofu, cut into small cubes
400 g (14 oz) mesclun leaves
1 Lebanese (short) cucumber, finely sliced
250 g (9 oz) cherry tomatoes, halved
2 teaspoons soy bean oil, extra

DRESSING

2 teaspoons white miso paste (see NOTE)
2 tablespoons mirin
1 teaspoon sesame oil
1 teaspoon grated fresh ginger
1 teaspoon finely snipped chives
1 tablespoon toasted sesame seeds

NUTRITION PER SERVE
Protein 12 g; Fat 8 g; Carbohydrate 4 g; Dietary Fibre 4 g; Cholesterol 0 mg; 590 kJ (140 Cal)

1 Mix together the light soy sauce, soy bean oil, garlic, ginger, chilli paste and ½ teaspoon salt in a bowl. Add the tofu and mix until well coated. Marinate for at least 10 minutes, or preferably overnight. Drain and reserve the marinade.

2 To make the dressing, combine the miso with 125 ml (4 fl oz/½ cup) hot water and leave until the miso dissolves. Add the mirin, sesame oil, ginger, chives and sesame seeds and stir until beginning to thicken.

3 Put the mesclun leaves, cucumber and tomato in a serving bowl.

4 Heat the extra soy bean oil on a chargrill plate or flat plate. Add the tofu and cook over medium heat for 4 minutes, or until golden brown. Pour on the reserved marinade and cook for a further 1 minute over high heat. Remove from the grill and cool for 5 minutes.

5 Add the tofu to the salad, drizzle with the dressing and toss well.

NOTE: *Miso is Japanese bean paste and is commonly used in soups, dressings, on grilled foods and as a flavouring for pickles.*

Gently stir the tofu cubes through the marinade until well coated.

Stir the dressing ingredients together until it begins to thicken.

Cook the tofu cubes over medium heat until each side is golden brown.

Roast pumpkin and onion with rocket

PREPARATION TIME: 8 MINUTES | TOTAL COOKING TIME: 35 MINUTES | SERVES 4

800 g (1 lb 12 oz) peeled jap pumpkin (winter squash)
2 small red onions
2 garlic cloves, finely chopped
cooking oil spray
150 g (5½ oz) rocket (arugula)
balsamic vinegar, to drizzle

1 Preheat the oven to 200°C (400°F/Gas 6).

2 Cut the pumpkin into 3 cm (1¼ inch) cubes and the onions into small wedges. Line a small baking dish with baking paper, add the vegetables and sprinkle with the garlic. Lightly spray with oil. Season and cook for 30–35 minutes, or until the pumpkin is just tender. Set aside.

3 Tear the leaves from the rocket into pieces. Arrange on a platter, then top with the pumpkin and onion. Drizzle all over with the balsamic vinegar. Serve warm.

NUTRITION PER SERVE
Protein 5.5 g; Fat 1 g; Carbohydrate 15 g; Dietary Fibre 4 g; Cholesterol 0 mg; 400 kJ (95 Cal)

Add the vegetables to a small baking dish with baking paper and sprinkle with garlic.

Tandoori lamb salad

PREPARATION TIME: 20 MINUTES + OVERNIGHT MARINATING | TOTAL COOKING TIME: 15 MINUTES | SERVES 4

250 g (9 oz/1 cup) low-fat plain yoghurt
2 garlic cloves, crushed
2 teaspoons grated fresh ginger
2 teaspoons ground turmeric
2 teaspoons garam masala
¼ teaspoon paprika
2 teaspoons ground coriander
red food colouring (optional)
500 g (1 lb 2 oz) lean lamb fillets
4 tablespoons lemon juice
1½ teaspoons chopped coriander (cilantro)
1 teaspoon chopped mint
150 g (5½ oz) mixed salad leaves
1 large mango, cut into strips
2 Lebanese (short) cucumbers, cut into strips

1 Mix the yoghurt, garlic, ginger and spices in a bowl, add a little colouring (if using) and toss with the lamb to thoroughly coat. Cover and refrigerate overnight.

2 Grill the lamb on a foil-lined baking tray under high heat for 7 minutes each side, or until the marinade starts to brown. Set aside for 5 minutes before serving.

3 Mix the lemon juice, coriander and mint, then season. Toss with the salad leaves, mango and cucumber, then arrange on plates. Slice the lamb and serve over the salad.

Coat the lamb with the marinade, cover and refrigerate overnight.

Cut the mango flesh into long, thin strips, using a sharp knife.

NUTRITION PER SERVE
Protein 30 g; Fat 6.5 g; Carbohydrate 8 g; Dietary Fibre 2 g; Cholesterol 90 mg; 965 kJ (230 Cal)

Thai beef salad with mint and coriander

PREPARATION TIME: 40 MINUTES | TOTAL COOKING TIME: 4 MINUTES | SERVES 6

2 tablespoons dried shrimp
125 g (4½ oz) English spinach
1 tablespoon sesame oil
500 g (1 lb 2 oz) rump steak
90 g (3¼ oz/1 cup) bean sprouts, trimmed
1 small red onion, thinly sliced
1 small red capsicum (pepper), cut into thin strips
1 small Lebanese (short) cucumber, cut into thin strips
200 g (7 oz) daikon radish, peeled and cut into thin strips
1 small tomato, halved, seeded and thinly sliced
1 handful mint leaves
1 very large handful coriander (cilantro) leaves
2 garlic cloves, finely chopped
1–2 small red chillies, chopped
2 small green chillies, chopped

DRESSING
3 tablespoons lime juice
3 tablespoons fish sauce
1 tablespoon finely chopped lemongrass
1 teaspoon sugar

1 Soak the dried shrimp in hot water for 15 minutes; drain well and chop finely. Wash the English spinach and drain well. Trim the thick stalks and coarsely shred the leaves.

2 Heat the oil in a frying pan, add the steak and cook over high heat for 1½–2 minutes on each side until medium-rare. Allow to cool slightly and then slice the steak thinly.

3 To make the dressing, combine the lime juice, fish sauce, lemongrass and sugar in a small bowl. Whisk until the ingredients are well combined.

4 To assemble the salad, combine the shrimp, sliced beef, bean sprouts, onion, capsicum, cucumber, radish, tomato, mint, coriander garlic and chillies in a large bowl. Place the spinach on a serving plate, top with the combined beef and vegetables, and drizzle with the dressing.

NUTRITION PER SERVE
Protein 25 g; Fat 6 g; Carbohydrate 6 g; Dietary Fibre 4 g; Cholesterol 65 mg; 730 kJ (175 Cal)

Slice the onion, and cut the capsicum, cucumber and radish into thin strips.

Trim the thick stalks from the English spinach and coarsely shred the leaves.

Cook the steak over high heat for a couple of minutes until it is medium-rare.

Chicken and cabbage salad

PREPARATION TIME: 15 MINUTES | TOTAL COOKING TIME: 10 MINUTES | SERVES 4

3 boneless, skinless chicken breasts
1 red chilli, seeded and finely chopped
3 tablespoons lime juice
2 tablespoons soft brown sugar
3 tablespoons fish sauce
½ Chinese cabbage, shredded
2 carrots, grated
50 g (1¾ oz/1 bunch) shredded mint

1 Put the chicken in a saucepan, cover with water and bring to the boil, then reduce the heat and simmer for 10 minutes, or until cooked through.

2 While the chicken is cooking, mix together the chilli, lime juice, sugar and fish sauce. Remove the chicken from the water. Cool slightly, then shred into small pieces.

3 Combine the chicken, cabbage, carrot, mint and dressing. Toss well and serve immediately.

NUTRITION PER SERVE
Protein 30 g; Fat 3 g; Carbohydrate 15 g; Dietary Fibre 3.5 g; Cholesterol 62 mg; 900 kJ (215 Cal)

Poach the chicken in the simmering water until it is cooked through.

Mix together the chilli, lime juice, sugar and fish sauce to make a dressing.

Mix together the chicken, cabbage, carrot, mint and dressing and toss well.

Chargrilled tuna and ruby grapefruit salad

PREPARATION TIME: 20 MINUTES | TOTAL COOKING TIME: 10 MINUTES | SERVES 6

4 ruby grapefruit
cooking oil spray
3 tuna steaks
150 g (5½ oz) rocket (arugula) leaves
1 red onion, sliced

DRESSING
2 tablespoons almond oil
2 tablespoons raspberry vinegar
½ teaspoon sugar
1 tablespoon shredded mint

1 Cut a slice off each end of the grapefruit and peel away the skin, removing all the pith. Separate the segments and set aside in a bowl.

2 Heat a barbecue grill plate or flat plate and spray lightly with oil. Cook each tuna steak for 3–4 minutes on each side. This will leave the centre slightly pink. Cool, then thinly slice.

3 To make the dressing, put the almond oil, vinegar, sugar and mint in a small screw-top jar and shake until well combined.

4 Place the rocket on a serving plate and top with the grapefruit segments, then the tuna and onion. Drizzle with the dressing and serve.

NUTRITION PER SERVE
Protein 15 g; Fat 7 g; Carbohydrate 8 g; Dietary Fibre 2 g; Cholesterol 50 mg; 1015 kJ (240 Cal)

Cut a slice off the ends of the grapefruit and peel away the skin and pith.

Separate the grapefruit into segments and set aside in a bowl.

Cook the tuna steaks on a lightly oiled grill plate—they should still be pink n the centre.

Pesto beef salad

PREPARATION TIME: 30 MINUTES | TOTAL COOKING TIME: 25 MINUTES | SERVES 8 AS A STARTER

100 g (3½ oz) button mushrooms
1 large yellow capsicum (pepper)
1 large red capsicum (pepper)
cooking oil spray
100 g (3½ oz) lean fillet steak
135 g (4¾ oz/1½ cups) penne

PESTO

3 very large handfuls basil leaves, plus extra, to serve
2 garlic cloves, chopped
2 tablespoons pepitas (pumpkin seeds)
1 tablespoon olive oil
2 tablespoons orange juice
1 tablespoon lemon juice

NUTRITION PER SERVE
Protein 8 g; Fat 5 g; Carbohydrate 15 g; Dietary Fibre 2 g; Cholesterol 7 mg; 660 kJ (135 Cal)

1 Cut the mushrooms into quarters. Cut the capsicums into large flat pieces, removing the seeds and membrane. Place skin side up under a hot grill (broiler) until blackened. Leave covered with a tea towel (dish towel) until cool, then peel away the skin and chop the flesh.

2 Spray a non-stick frying pan with oil and cook the steak over high heat for 3–4 minutes each side until it is medium-rare. Remove and leave for 5 minutes before cutting into thin slices. Season with a little salt.

3 To make the pesto, finely chop the basil leaves, garlic and pepitas in a food processor. With the motor running, add the oil, orange and lemon juice. Season well.

4 Meanwhile, cook the penne in a large pan of rapidly boiling salted water until *al dente*. Drain, then toss with the pesto in a large bowl.

5 Add the capsicum pieces, steak slices, mushroom quarters and basil leaves to the penne and toss to distribute evenly. Serve immediately.

When the capsicum has cooled, peel away the skin and dice the flesh.

Cook the steak in a non-stick frying pan until it is medium-rare.

Add the oil with the orange and lemon juice, in a thin stream.

Spicy pork salad

PREPARATION TIME: 20 MINUTES + 3 HOURS MARINATING | TOTAL COOKING TIME: 15 MINUTES | SERVES 6

1 tablespoon oil
500 g (1 lb 2 oz) minced (ground) pork
2 tablespoons fish sauce
1 tablespoon soy sauce
2½ tablespoons lime juice
1 tablespoon soft brown sugar
10 spring onions (scallions), finely chopped
3 lemongrass stems, white part only, finely chopped
2 red chillies, seeded and sliced
2 tablespoons each of chopped coriander, mint and parsley
lettuce leaves, for serving

1 Heat the oil in a frying pan. Add the minced pork and cook over medium–high heat for 10 minutes, or until well browned, breaking up any lumps with a fork as it cooks. Remove from the pan and leave to cool.

2 Combine the sauces, lime juice and brown sugar in a bowl. Add the pork. Mix in the spring onion, lemongrass, chilli and fresh herbs.

3 Cover and refrigerate for at least 3 hours, stirring occasionally, or overnight. To serve, lay a lettuce leaf on each plate and spoon in some of the pork mixture.

NUTRITION PER SERVE

Protein 20 g; Fat 10 g; Carbohydrate 5 g; Dietary Fibre 0 g; Cholesterol 50 mg; 875 kJ (210 Cal)

Chop the spring onions, lemongrass, chillies, coriander, mint and parsley.

Break up any lumps of the minced pork with a fork as you brown it.

Mix in the spring onion, lemongrass, chilli and herbs and leave to marinate.

Lime and prawn salad

PREPARATION TIME: 35 MINUTES | TOTAL COOKING TIME: 2 MINUTES | SERVES 4

200 g (7 oz) baby green beans
2 Lebanese (short) cucumbers, sliced
4 spring onions (scallions), finely chopped
1 tablespoon finely shredded makrut (kaffir lime) leaves
15 g (½ oz/¼ cup) flaked coconut
750 g (1 lb 10 oz) cooked prawns (shrimp), peeled and deveined, tails intact
2 teaspoons shredded lime zest

DRESSING

1 tablespoon peanut oil
1 tablespoon nam pla (Thai fish sauce)
1 tablespoon grated palm sugar (jaggery)
1 tablespoon chopped coriander (cilantro)
2 teaspoons soy sauce
1–2 teaspoons sweet chilli sauce
3 tablespoons lime juice

1 Cook the beans in a small saucepan of boiling water for 2 minutes. Drain and cover with cold water, then drain again and pat dry with paper towels.

2 To make the dressing, whisk all the ingredients in a bowl.

3 Combine the beans, cucumber, spring onion, makrut leaves, flaked coconut and prawns in a large bowl. Add the dressing and toss gently to combine. Place the salad in a large serving bowl and garnish with the shredded lime zest.

NOTE: *Young lemon leaves can be used in place of the makrut leaves if the makrut leaves are not available. Soft brown or dark brown sugar may be substituted for the palm sugar.*

Cut the cucumbers in half lengthways, then cut into slices.

Put the beans into a small saucepan of boiling water and cook for 2 minutes.

NUTRITION PER SERVE
Protein 45 g; Fat 8 g; Carbohydrate 7 g; Dietary Fibre 3 g; Cholesterol 350 mg; 1200 kJ (285 Cal)

Thai-spiced pork and green mango salad

PREPARATION TIME: 45 MINUTES + 2 HOURS REFRIGERATION | TOTAL COOKING TIME: 10 MINUTES | SERVES 4

2 stems lemongrass (white part only), thinly sliced
1 garlic clove
2 red Asian shallots (eschalots)
1 tablespoon coarsely chopped fresh ginger
1 red bird's eye chilli, seeded
1 tablespoon fish sauce
1 large handful coriander (cilantro)
1 teaspoon grated lime zest
1 tablespoon lime juice
2 tablespoons oil
2 pork tenderloins, trimmed

DRESSING
1 large red chilli, seeded and finely chopped
2 garlic cloves, finely chopped
3 coriander (cilantro) roots, finely chopped
1¼ tablespoons grated palm sugar (jaggery)
2 tablespoons fish sauce
3 tablespoons lime juice

SALAD
2 green mangoes or 1 small green papaya, peeled, pitted and cut into matchsticks
1 carrot, grated
45 g (1½ oz/½ cup) bean sprouts, trimmed
½ red onion, thinly sliced
3 tablespoons roughly chopped mint
3 tablespoons roughly chopped coriander (cilantro) leaves
3 tablespoons roughly chopped Vietnamese mint

1 Place the lemongrass, garlic, shallots, ginger, chilli, fish sauce, coriander, lime zest, lime juice and oil in a blender or food processor and process until a coarse paste forms. Transfer to a non-metallic dish. Coat the pork in the marinade, cover and refrigerate for at least 2 hours, but no longer than 4 hours.

2 To make the salad dressing, mix all the ingredients together in a bowl.

3 Combine all the salad ingredients in a large bowl.

4 Preheat a grill (broiler) or a chargrill pan and cook the pork over medium heat for 4–5 minutes each side, or until cooked through. Remove from the heat, and then leave to rest for 5 minutes before slicing to serve.

5 Toss the dressing and salad together. Season to taste with salt and cracked black pepper. Arrange the sliced pork in a circle in the centre of each plate and top with salad. Delicious with steamed jasmine rice.

NUTRITION PER SERVE
Protein 60 g; Fat 14 g; Carbohydrate 20 g; Dietary Fibre 3 g; Cholesterol 122 mg; 1860 kJ (444 Cal)

Mix the marinade ingredients to a coarse paste in a processor or blender.

Cook the pork under the grill (broiler) or in a chargrill pan until it is cooked through.

Citrus fruit and rocket salad

PREPARATION TIME: 20 MINUTES | TOTAL COOKING TIME: NIL | SERVES 6

1 grapefruit
2 small red grapefruit
4 oranges
1 red onion, sliced
1 large handful coriander (cilantro) leaves
2 tablespoons honey
4 tablespoons raspberry vinegar
150 g (5½ oz) rocket (arugula)

1 Remove the zest from the grapefruits and oranges. Remove and discard all the pith from a few slices of the zest from each fruit and cut the zest into long thin strips. Remove any remaining pith from the fruit and slice between each section. Segment the fruit over a bowl to catch any juice, then set the juice aside.

2 Put the segments and zest in a salad bowl with the onion and coriander leaves. Add the honey and raspberry vinegar to the reserved fruit juice and whisk to combine. Pour over the salad and toss. Serve on a bed of rocket.

NUTRITION PER SERVE
Protein 3 g; Fat 0 g; Carbohydrate 25 g; Dietary Fibre 3.5 g; Cholesterol 0 mg; 505 kJ (120 Cal)

Remove and discard all the pith from the zest of each fruit.

Melon and pineapple with chilli syrup

PREPARATION TIME: 15 MINUTES | TOTAL COOKING TIME: 20 MINUTES | SERVES 4

JALAPEÑO SYRUP
125 ml (4 fl oz/½ cup) lime juice
110 g (3¾ oz/½ cup) sugar
2 jalapeño chillies, stems removed, sliced into thin rounds, plus extra, to serve

½ small round watermelon, cut into small cubes
1 small ripe pineapple, peeled and cut into small triangles
mint sprigs, to serve

1 To make the jalapeño syrup, stir the lime juice, sugar and 125 ml (4 fl oz/½ cup) water in a small pan over low–medium heat without boiling until the sugar has completely dissolved. Bring to the boil, then simmer for 10–15 minutes, without stirring, or until thick and syrupy.

2 Add the chilli, cook for 5 minutes and cool to room temperature.

3 Arrange the fruit on a plate; drizzle with the syrup. Garnish with the mint and extra chilli slices. Serve chilled.

NUTRITION PER SERVE
Protein 2 g; Fat 0 g; Carbohydrate 45 g; Dietary Fibre 3 g; Cholesterol 0 mg; 745 kJ (180 Cal)

Peel and slice the pineapple and cut the slices into small triangles.

Simmer the syrup, without boiling, until all the sugar has dissolved.

Add the sliced jalapeño chilli to the syrup and cook for 5 minutes.

Japanese king prawn and noodle salad

PREPARATION TIME: 35 MINUTES | TOTAL COOKING TIME: 15 MINUTES | SERVES 6

500 g (1 lb 2 oz) fresh udon noodles
2 teaspoons sesame oil
3 garlic cloves, finely chopped
4 cm (1½ inch) piece ginger, finely chopped
200 g (7 oz) broccoli, cut into small pieces
2 carrots, cut into matchsticks
100 g (3½ oz) snow peas (mangetouts), sliced into long, thin strips
90 g (3¼ oz/1 cup) bean sprouts, trimmed
1 large handful coriander (cilantro), chopped
2 tablespoons mirin
3 tablespoons low-salt soy sauce
8 cooked king prawns (shrimp), peeled and deveined, tails intact
2 teaspoons sesame seeds, toasted
sliced spring onions (scallions), to garnish

NUTRITION PER SERVE
Protein 20 g; Fat 8 g; Carbohydrate 65 g; Dietary Fibre 8 g; Cholesterol 35 mg; 1690 kJ (405 Cal)

1 Cook the udon noodles in a large pan of boiling water for 5 minutes, or until tender. Drain and rinse in cold water to prevent them sticking together. Transfer to a large bowl and cut into small pieces, using scissors. Toss 1 teaspoon of the sesame oil through, cover and set aside.

2 Heat the remaining sesame oil in a small frying pan, add the garlic and ginger and cook over low heat for 5 minutes, stirring occasionally. Remove from the heat, cool and add to the noodles.

3 Bring a large saucepan of water to the boil and add the broccoli, carrot and snow peas. Return to the boil, reduce the heat and simmer for 1 minute. Rinse under cold water until the vegetables are cold. Drain.

4 Add the blanched vegetables, bean sprouts, coriander, mirin, soy sauce and prawns to the noodles. Toss together until well combined. Transfer to a serving bowl and sprinkle with sesame seeds and spring onion. Serve immediately.

NOTE: *Udon noodles and mirin are available from Japanese or Asian food stores and some supermarkets.*

Use scissors to cut the udon noodles into pieces so they are easier to eat.

Cook the garlic and ginger in the sesame oil for about 5 minutes.

Blanch the broccoli, carrot and snow peas, then rinse under water until completely cold.

Meat

Beef and vegetable casserole

PREPARATION TIME: 40 MINUTES | TOTAL COOKING TIME: 1 HOUR 40 MINUTES | SERVES 6

500 g (1 lb 2 oz) lean round steak
cooking oil spray
1 onion, sliced
3 garlic cloves, crushed
2 teaspoons ground cumin
1 teaspoon dried thyme leaves
2 bay leaves
400 g (14 oz) tin chopped tomatoes
500 g (1 lb 2 oz) potatoes, chopped
2 large carrots, thickly sliced
4 zucchini (courgettes), thickly sliced
250 g (9 oz) mushrooms, halved
250 g (9 oz) yellow squash, halved
2 tablespoons tomato paste (concentrated purée)
125 ml (4 fl oz/½ cup) red wine
3 large handfuls parsley, chopped

1 Preheat the oven to 180°C (350°F/Gas 4). Remove any excess fat and sinew from the meat and cut into 2 cm (¾ inch) cubes. Spray a deep, non-stick frying pan with oil and fry the meat in batches until brown. Remove from the pan. Spray the pan again, add the onion and cook until lightly golden. Add the garlic, cumin, thyme and bay leaves and stir for 1 minute.

2 Return the meat and any juices to the pan, tossing to coat with the spices. Add 375 ml (13 fl oz/1½ cups) water and the tomato, scraping the pan. Simmer for 10 minutes, or until thickened. Mix in a large casserole dish with the vegetables, tomato paste and wine.

3 Bake, covered, for 1 hour. Stir well, then uncover and bake for 20 minutes. Season, remove the bay leaves and stir in the parsley.

NUTRITION PER SERVE
Protein 25 g; Fat 4 g; Carbohydrate 20 g; Dietary Fibre 6.5 g; Cholesterol 50 mg; 930 kJ (220 Cal)

Discard any excess fat and sinew from the steak and cut the steak into cubes.

When the onion is golden, add the garlic, cumin, thyme and bay leaves.

Pour the wine into the casserole dish and mix through the vegetables with the tomato paste.

Madras beef curry

PREPARATION TIME: 20 MINUTES | TOTAL COOKING TIME: 1 HOUR 40 MINUTES | SERVES 4

1 kg (2 lb 4 oz) skirt or chuck steak
1 tablespoon oil
1 onion, chopped
3–4 tablespoons Madras curry paste
60 g (2¼ oz/¼ cup) tomato paste (concentrated purée)
250 ml (9 fl oz/1 cup) beef stock

1 Trim the meat of any fat or sinew and cut it into bite-sized cubes. Heat the oil in a large frying pan, add the onion and cook over medium heat for 10 minutes, or until browned.

2 Add the curry paste and stir for 1 minute, or until fragrant. Then add the meat and cook, stirring, until coated with the curry paste. Stir in the tomato paste and stock. Reduce the heat and simmer, covered, for 1 hour 15 minutes. Uncover and simmer for 15 minutes, or until the meat is tender.

STORAGE TIME: *This dish can be refrigerated for 2–3 days.*

NUTRITION PER SERVE
Protein 53 g; Fat 15 g; Carbohydrate 4.5 g; Dietary Fibre 1.5 g; Cholesterol 170 mg; 1514 kJ (362 Cal)

Trim the meat of any excess fat or sinew and cut into cubes.

Cook the chopped onion in a large frying pan until it is browned.

Add the meat to the pan and stir until coated with the curry paste.

Navarin of lamb

PREPARATION TIME: 20 MINUTES | TOTAL COOKING TIME: 1 HOUR 45 MINUTES | SERVES 4

1.25 kg (2 lb 12 oz) boned shoulder or leg of lamb (ask your butcher to bone the meat)
1 tablespoon oil
1 small onion, quartered
1 garlic clove, crushed
2 bacon slices, rind removed, finely chopped
12 large bulb spring onions (scallions), stems removed
1 tablespoon plain (all-purpose) flour
250 ml (9 fl oz/1 cup) chicken stock
1 tablespoon tomato paste (concentrated purée)
1 turnip, swede (rutabaga) or parsnip, peeled and cubed
1 large carrot, thickly sliced
4–6 new potatoes, halved
60 g (2¼ oz/½ cup) frozen peas

1 Remove any excess fat from the lamb and cut the meat into bite-sized cubes. Preheat the oven to 150°C (300°F/Gas 2). Heat the oil in a heavy-based non-stick saucepan. Cook the onion, garlic, bacon and spring onions over medium heat for 5 minutes, or until the onion is soft. Remove with a slotted spoon to a large heatproof casserole dish.

2 Add the lamb to the saucepan and brown quickly in batches. When all the meat is browned return it to the pan and sprinkle with the flour. Stir for 1 minute to combine, then pour on the stock and tomato paste. Stir until thickened and smooth and pour into the casserole.

3 Stir in the turnip, swede or parsnip, carrot and potato. Cover with a tight-fitting lid and bake for 1¼ hours, stirring a couple of times. Add the peas and cook for another 15 minutes, or until the lamb is tender. Season to taste before serving.

NUTRITION PER SERVE
Protein 9 g; Fat 12 g; Carbohydrate 22 g; Dietary Fibre 7 g; Cholesterol 30 mg; 970 kJ (235 Cal)

Remove the onion, spring onions, garlic and bacon to a casserole dish.

Return all the browned meat to the pan and sprinkle with flour.

Pork, beer and chickpea stew

PREPARATION TIME: 35 MINUTES | TOTAL COOKING TIME: 1 HOUR 30 MINUTES | SERVES 4

2 teaspoons ground cumin
1 teaspoon ground coriander
½ teaspoon chilli powder
¼ teaspoon ground cinnamon
400 g (14 oz) lean diced pork, trimmed
1 tablespoon plain (all-purpose) flour
1 tablespoon olive oil
1 large onion, finely chopped
3 garlic cloves, finely chopped
2 large carrots, finely chopped
2 celery stalks, thinly sliced
125 ml (4 fl oz/½ cup) chicken stock
125 ml (4 fl oz/½ cup) beer
2 ripe tomatoes, chopped
310 g (11 oz) tin chickpeas, rinsed
2 tablespoons chopped parsley

1 Cook the spices in a dry frying pan over low heat, shaking the pan, for 1 minute, or until aromatic.

2 Combine the pork with the spices and flour in a plastic bag and toss well. Remove the pork and shake off the excess flour. Heat the oil in a large heavy-based saucepan over high heat and cook the pork, tossing regularly, for 8 minutes, or until lightly browned.

3 Add the onion, garlic, carrot, celery and half the stock to the pan and toss well. Cover and cook for 10 minutes. Add the remaining stock, beer and tomato and season to taste. Bring to the boil, reduce the heat, cover with a tight-fitting lid, then simmer over low heat for 1 hour. Gently shake the pan occasionally, but do not remove the lid during cooking. Stir in the chickpeas and parsley. Simmer, uncovered, for 5 minutes and serve.

NUTRITION PER SERVE
Protein 40 g; Fat 10 g; Carbohydrate 35 g; Dietary Fibre 15 g; Cholesterol 50 mg; 1720 kJ (410 Cal

Chop the carrots into small pieces and thinly slice the celery stalks.

Dry-fry the spices over low heat, stirring the spices and shaking the pan.

Cook the flour-coated pork, tossing regularly, until lightly browned.

Slow-cooked lamb shanks

PREPARATION TIME: 20 MINUTES | TOTAL COOKING TIME: 3 HOURS | SERVES 4

1 tablespoon oil
4 lamb shanks
2 red onions, sliced
10 garlic cloves
400 g (14 oz) tin chopped tomatoes
125 ml (4 fl oz/½ cup) dry white wine
1 bay leaf
1 teaspoon grated lemon zest
1 large red capsicum (pepper), chopped
3 tablespoons chopped parsley

1 Preheat the oven to 170°C (325°F/Gas 3). Heat the oil in a large ovenproof casserole dish, add the shanks in batches and cook over high heat for 8–10 minutes, or until browned on all sides. Return all the lamb to the casserole.

2 Add the onion and garlic to the casserole and cook until softened. Add the tomato, wine, bay leaf, lemon zest, capsicum and 125 ml (4 fl oz/½ cup) water and bring to the boil.

3 Cover the casserole and cook in the oven for 2–2½ hours, or until the meat is tender and falling off the bone and the sauce has thickened. Season to taste. Sprinkle the parsley over the top before serving. Serve with couscous or soft polenta.

NUTRITION PER SERVE
Protein 35 g; Fat 10 g; Carbohydrate 9 g; Dietary Fibre 4.5 g; Cholesterol 85 mg; 1275 kJ (305 Cal)

Add the shanks in batches to a large flamefroof casserole dish.

Add the onion and garlic to the casserole and cook until softened.

Add the tomato, wine, bay leaf, lemon zest, capsicum and water.

Burmese pork curry

PREPARATION TIME: 30 MINUTES | TOTAL COOKING TIME: 1 HOUR | SERVES 6

2 lemongrass stems, white part only, sliced
1 red onion, chopped
1 garlic clove
1 teaspoon grated fresh ginger
2 large red dried chillies
1 teaspoon fenugreek seeds, roasted and ground
1 teaspoon yellow mustard seeds, roasted and ground
2 teaspoons paprika
2 tablespoons worcestershire sauce
750 g (1 lb 10 oz) lean boneless shoulder of pork, cut into cubes
2 tablespoons fish sauce
6 new potatoes, peeled and sliced
2 small red onions, diced
1 tablespoon olive oil
2 tablespoons mango chutney

1 Put the lemongrass, onion, garlic, ginger, chillies, seeds, paprika and sauce in a processor or blender and mix to a thick paste.

2 Place the pork in a bowl, sprinkle with the fish sauce and ¼ teaspoon ground black pepper.

3 Place the potato and onion in another bowl, add 3 tablespoons of the paste and toss to coat. Add the remaining paste to the pork. Mix well.

4 Heat the oil in a frying pan or wok over medium heat. Add the pork and cook in batches, stirring, for 8 minutes, or until the meat begins to brown. Remove from the pan. Add the potato and onion and cook, stirring, for 5 minutes, or until soft and starting to brown.

5 Return the meat to the pan and stir in 750 ml (26 fl oz/3 cups) water, adding 250 ml (9 fl oz/1 cup) at a time. Stir in the mango chutney, then reduce the heat and simmer for 30 minutes.

NUTRITION PER SERVE
Protein 30 g; Fat 8.5 g; Carbohydrate 16 g; Dietary Fibre 2.5 g; Cholesterol 60 mg; 1126 kJ (270 Cal)

Process all the spice paste ingredients to make a thick paste.

Heat the oil in a frying pan or wok and brown the pork in batches.

Veal cutlets in chilli tomato sauce

PREPARATION TIME: 35 MINUTES | TOTAL COOKING TIME: 35 MINUTES | SERVES 4

5 slices wholemeal (whole-wheat) bread
3 tablespoons parsley
3 garlic cloves
4 thick veal cutlets, trimmed
3 tablespoons skim milk
2 teaspoons olive oil
1 onion, finely chopped
1 tablespoon capers, drained and well rinsed
1 teaspoon tinned green peppercorns, chopped
1 teaspoon chopped red chilli
2 tablespoons balsamic vinegar
1 teaspoon soft brown sugar
2 tablespoons tomato paste (concentrated purée)
440 g (15½ oz) tin chopped tomatoes

NUTRITION PER SERVE
Protein 15 g; Fat 6 g; Carbohydrate 20 g; Dietary Fibre 5 g; Cholesterol 25 mg; 845 kJ (200 Cal)

1 Preheat the oven to 180°C (350°F/Gas 4). Place a rack in a small baking dish. Chop the bread, parsley and garlic in a food processor to make fine breadcrumbs.

2 Season the cutlets on both sides with salt and black pepper. Pour the milk into a bowl and put the breadcrumbs on a plate. Dip the veal in the milk, then coat in the crumbs, pressing the crumbs on. Transfer to the rack and bake for 20 minutes.

3 While the veal is cooking, heat the oil in a small saucepan over medium heat. Add the onion, capers, peppercorns and chilli, cover and cook for 8 minutes. Mix in the vinegar, sugar and tomato paste and stir until boiling. Stir in the tomato, reduce the heat and simmer for 15 minutes.

4 Remove the cutlets from the rack and wipe the dish. Place the tomato sauce in the base and put the cutlets on top, and return to the oven. Reduce the oven to 150°C (300°F/Gas 2) and bake for 10 minutes to heat through.

Trim the veal cutlets of any excess fat and gristle and then season with salt and pepper.

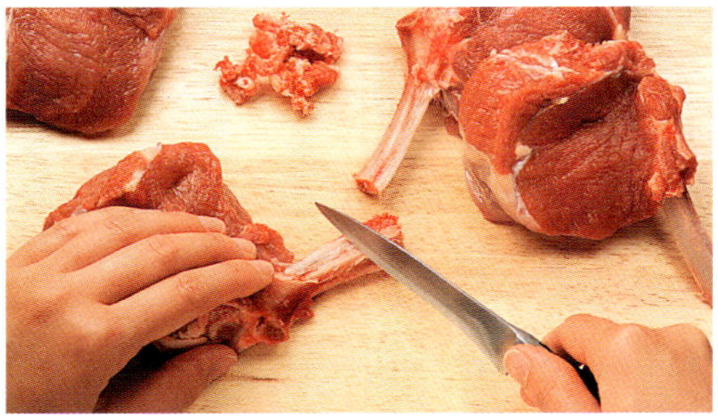

Dip the seasoned cutlets in the milk, then press into the breadcrumb mixture.

Put the cutlets on top of the tomato sauce, then return to the oven.

2006
GEORGES DUBŒUF

Linguine with bacon, mushrooms and peas

PREPARATION TIME: 20 MINUTES | TOTAL COOKING TIME: 25 MINUTES | SERVES 4

3 bacon slices
2 teaspoons olive oil
2–3 garlic cloves, crushed
1 red onion, chopped
185 g (6½ oz) field mushrooms, sliced
2 large handfuls parsley, chopped
155 g (5½ oz/1 cup) peas
375 ml (13 fl oz/1½ cups) low-fat evaporated milk
2 teaspoons cornflour (cornstarch)
325 g (11½ oz) dried linguine
25 g (1 oz) parmesan cheese shavings (optional)

1 Remove the fat and rind from the bacon and chop roughly. Heat the oil in a medium frying pan, add the garlic, onion and bacon and cook over low heat for 5 minutes, stirring frequently, until the onion and bacon are soft. Add the sliced mushrooms and cook, stirring, for another 5 minutes, or until soft.

2 Add the parsley, peas and milk to the pan. Mix the cornflour with 1 tablespoon of water until smooth, add to the mixture and stir over medium heat until slightly thickened.

3 Meanwhile, cook the pasta in a large pan of rapidly boiling, salted water for 8 minutes, or until *al dente*. Drain and serve with the hot sauce and parmesan shavings, if desired.

Discard the fat and rind from the bacon and chop the meat roughly into strips.

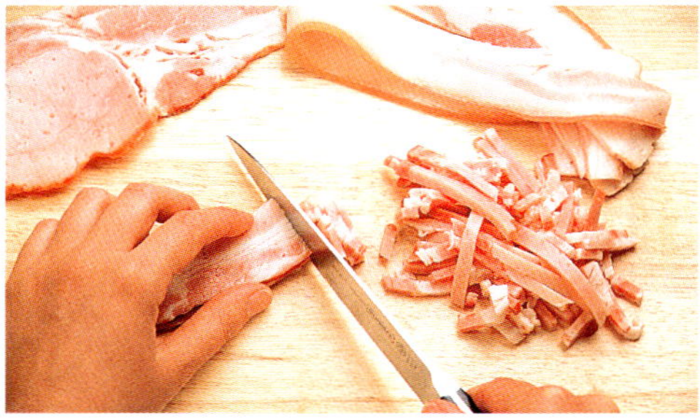

When the onion is softened, add the sliced mushrooms and stir while cooking.

NUTRITION PER SERVE
Protein 30 g; Fat 7 g; Carbohydrate 80 g; Dietary Fibre 9 g; Cholesterol 25 mg; 2085 kJ (500 Cal)

Pork and apple braise

PREPARATION TIME: 20 MINUTES | TOTAL COOKING TIME: 40 MINUTES | SERVES 4

1 tablespoon oil
1 large onion, thinly sliced
1 garlic clove, chopped
2 teaspoons soft brown sugar
2 green apples, cut into wedges
4 pork loin steaks or medallions
2 tablespoons brandy
2 tablespoons seeded mustard
250 ml (90 fl oz/1 cup) chicken stock
140 g (5 oz/⅔ cup) pitted prunes
125 ml (4 fl oz/½ cup) light pouring (whipping) cream

1 Heat the oil in a large heavy-based saucepan. Cook the onion and garlic for 10 minutes over low heat, stirring often, until softened and golden brown. Add the sugar and apple and cook, stirring regularly, until the apple begins to brown. Remove the apple and onion from the pan.

2 Reheat the pan and lightly brown the pork steaks, two at a time, then return them all to the pan. Add the brandy and stir until it has nearly all evaporated. Add the mustard and stock. Simmer over low heat, covered, for 15 minutes.

3 Return the apple to the pan with the prunes and cream and simmer for 10 minutes, or until the pork is tender. Season to taste before serving.

HINT: *Take care not to overcook pork or it can become tough and dry.*

NUTRITION PER SERVE
Protein 25 g; Fat 12 g; Carbohydrate 22 g; Dietary Fibre 4 g; Cholesterol 55 mg; 1250 kJ (298 Cal)

Stir the apple regularly over the heat until it begins to brown.

Brown the pork steaks two at a time and then return them all to the pan.

Indian-style lamb couscous

PREPARATION TIME: 25 MINUTES | TOTAL COOKING TIME: 35 MINUTES | SERVES 6

250 g (9 oz) lamb backstrap (tender eye fillet of the lamb loin)
1 tablespoon mild curry powder
2 tablespoons pepitas (pumpkin seeds)
2 tablespoons sesame seeds
2 teaspoons cumin seeds
2 teaspoons coriander seeds
1 tablespoon oil
2 tablespoons lemon juice, plus extra, to serve
1 onion, chopped
1 carrot, chopped
125 g (4½ oz) orange sweet potato, cubed
1 garlic clove, finely chopped
185 g (6½ oz/1 cup) couscous
40 g (1½ oz/⅓ cup) raisins

NUTRITION PER SERVE
Protein 15 g; Fat 10 g; Carbohydrate 30 g; Dietary Fibre 3 g; Cholesterol 30 mg; 1135 kJ (270 Cal)

1 Sprinkle the lamb with the combined curry powder and a pinch of salt, then turn to coat well. Cover with plastic wrap and refrigerate.

2 Place the pepitas and sesame seeds in a dry frying pan and cook, stirring, over medium–high heat until the seeds begin to brown. Add the cumin and coriander seeds and continue stirring until the pepitas are puffed up. Remove from the heat and allow to cool.

3 Heat the oil in a frying pan, add the lamb and cook over medium–high heat for 5–8 minutes, or until browned. Remove from the pan, drizzle with half the lemon and leave to cool to room temperature. Turn the meat occasionally to coat in the juice while cooling.

4 Using the same pan, stir the onion, carrot and sweet potato over high heat until the onion is translucent. Reduce the heat to medium, add 3 tablespoons water, cover and cook for about 3 minutes, or until the vegetables are tender. Stir in the garlic and remaining lemon juice.

5 Pour 250 ml (9 fl oz/1 cup) boiling water into a heatproof bowl and add the couscous. Stir until combined. Leave for about 2 minutes, or until the water has been absorbed. Fluff gently with a fork to separate the grains. Add the vegetable mixture, raisins and most of the toasted seeds, reserving some to sprinkle over the top, and toss until just combined. Spoon the mixture onto a serving plate. Slice the lamb thinly and arrange over the mixture. Drizzle with the extra lemon juice and sprinkle with the seeds.

Sprinkle the lamb backstrap with the combined curry powder and salt.

Fry the seeds in a dry frying pan until the pepitas puff up.

When the water has been absorbed, fluff the couscous gently with a fork.

Penne with bacon, ricotta and basil

PREPARATION TIME: 20 MINUTES | TOTAL COOKING TIME: 15 MINUTES | SERVES 4

2 bacon slices
2 teaspoons olive oil
2–3 garlic cloves, crushed
1 onion, finely chopped
2 spring onions (scallions), finely chopped
250 g (9 oz/1 cup) ricotta cheese
1 very large handful basil, finely chopped
325 g (11½ oz/3⅔ cups) penne
8 cherry tomatoes, halved

1 Remove the fat and rind from the bacon and chop roughly. Heat the oil in a frying pan, add the bacon, garlic, onion and spring onion and stir over medium heat for 5 minutes, or until cooked. Remove from the heat, stir in the ricotta and chopped basil and beat until smooth.

2 Meanwhile, cook the pasta in a large saucepan of rapidly boiling salted water for 10 minutes, or until *al dente*. Just prior to draining the pasta, add about 250 ml (9 fl oz/1 cup) of the pasta water to the ricotta mixture to thin the sauce. Add more water if you prefer an even thinner sauce. Season well.

3 Drain the pasta and stir the sauce and tomato halves into the pasta.

NUTRITION PER SERVE
Protein 20 g; Fat 10 g; Carbohydrate 65 g; Dietary Fibre 5 g; Cholesterol 40 mg; 1885 kJ (450 Cal)

Remove the bacon mixture from the heat and stir in the ricotta and chopped basil.

Bring a large pan of salted water to a rapid boil before adding the pasta.

Thin the ricotta mixture with about 250 ml (9 fl oz/1 cup) of the water from the cooked pasta.

Rogan josh

PREPARATION TIME: 25 MINUTES | TOTAL COOKING TIME: 1 HOUR 40 MINUTES | SERVES 6

1 kg (2 lb 4 oz) boned leg of lamb
1 tablespoon oil
2 onions, chopped
125 g (4½ oz/½ cup) low-fat plain yoghurt
1 teaspoon chilli powder
1 tablespoon ground coriander
2 teaspoons ground cumin
1 teaspoon ground cardamom
½ teaspoon ground cloves
1 teaspoon ground turmeric
3 garlic cloves, crushed
1 tablespoon grated fresh ginger
400 g (14 oz) tin chopped tomatoes
30 g (1 oz/¼ cup) slivered almonds
1 teaspoon garam masala
chopped coriander (cilantro) leaves, for serving

1 Trim the lamb of any fat or sinew and cut into small cubes.

2 Heat the oil in a large saucepan, add the onion and cook, stirring, for 5 minutes, or until soft. Stir in the yoghurt, chilli powder, coriander, cumin, cardamom, cloves, turmeric, garlic and ginger. Add the tomato and 1 teaspoon salt and simmer for 5 minutes.

3 Add the lamb and stir until coated. Cover and cook over low heat, stirring occasionally, for 1–1½ hours, or until the lamb is tender. Uncover and simmer until the liquid thickens.

4 Meanwhile, toast the almonds in a dry frying pan over medium heat for 3–4 minutes, shaking the pan gently, until the nuts are golden. Remove from the pan at once to prevent them burning.

5 Add the garam masala to the curry and mix through well. Sprinkle the slivered almonds and coriander leaves over the top and serve.

NUTRITION PER SERVE
Protein 40 g; Fat 13 g; Carbohydrate 5.5 g; Dietary Fibre 2 g; Cholesterol 122 mg; 1236 kJ (295 Cal)

Cook the onion in the oil for 5 minutes, or until it is soft.

Toast the almonds in a dry frying pan until they are golden brown.

Moussaka

PREPARATION TIME: 30 MINUTES | TOTAL COOKING TIME: 1 HOUR 30 MINUTES | SERVES 6

1 kg (2 lb 4 oz) eggplants (aubergines)
cooking oil spray
400 g (14 oz) lean minced (ground) lamb
2 onions, finely chopped
2 garlic cloves, crushed
400 g (14 oz) tin tomatoes
1 tablespoon chopped thyme
1 teaspoon chopped oregano
1 tablespoon tomato paste (concentrated purée)
4 tablespoons dry white wine
1 bay leaf
1 teaspoon sugar

CHEESE SAUCE

310 ml (10¾ fl oz/1¼ cups) skim milk
2 tablespoons plain (all-purpose) flour
30 g (1 oz/¼ cup) grated reduced-fat cheddar cheese
250 g (9 oz/1 cup) ricotta cheese
pinch of cayenne pepper
¼ teaspoon ground nutmeg

NUTRITION PER SERVE
Protein 10 g; Fat 10 g; Carbohydrate 15 g; Dietary Fibre 5.5 g; Cholesterol 25 mg; 735 kJ (175 Cal)

1 Cut the eggplant into 1 cm (½ inch) thick slices, place in a colander over a large bowl, layering with a sprinkling of salt. Leave to stand for 20 minutes. Spray a non-stick frying pan with oil and brown the lamb over medium–high heat. Once all the meat is browned, set aside.

2 Spray the pan again with oil, add the onion and stir continuously for 2 minutes. Add 1 tablespoon water to prevent sticking. Add the garlic and cook for about 3 minutes. Push the undrained tomatoes through a sieve, then discard the contents of the sieve.

3 Return the meat to the pan with the onion. Add the fresh herbs, tomato pulp, paste, wine, bay leaf and sugar. Cover and simmer over low heat for 20 minutes.

4 Preheat a grill (broiler). Rinse and pat dry the eggplant, place on a grill tray, spray with oil and grill under high heat for 4–5 minutes, or until golden brown. Turn over, spray with oil and grill until golden brown. Arrange half the eggplant slices over the base of a 1.5 litre (52 fl oz/6 cup) capacity baking dish. Top with half the meat and then repeat the layers.

5 Preheat the oven to 180°C (350°F/Gas 4). To make the cheese sauce, blend a little of the milk with the flour in a small saucepan to form a paste. Gradually blend in the remaining milk, stirring constantly over low heat until the milk starts to simmer and thicken. Remove from the heat and stir in the remaining ingredients. Pour over the moussaka and bake for 35–40 minutes, or until the cheese is golden.

Sprinkle a generous amount of salt on the eggplant slices and set aside.

Rinse and dry the eggplant slices, then grill on both sides until golden.

Layer the eggplant slices and meat evenly in the baking dish.

Spaghetti bolognese

PREPARATION TIME: 30 MINUTES | TOTAL COOKING TIME: 1 HOUR 20 MINUTES | SERVES 6

cooking oil spray
2 onions, finely chopped
2 garlic cloves, finely chopped
2 carrots, finely chopped
2 celery stalks, finely chopped
400 g (14 oz) lean minced (ground) beef
1 kg (2 1b 4 oz) tomatoes, chopped
125 ml (4 fl oz/½ cup) dry red wine
350 g (12 oz) spaghetti
1 very large handful parsley, finely chopped

1 Lightly spray a large saucepan with oil. Place over medium heat and add the onion, garlic, carrot and celery. Stir for 5 minutes, or until the vegetables have softened. Add 1 tablespoon water, if necessary, to prevent sticking.

2 Increase the heat to high, add the minced beef and cook for 5 minutes, or until browned. Stir constantly to prevent the meat sticking. Add the tomato, wine and 250 ml (9 fl oz/1 cup) water. Bring to the boil, reduce the heat and simmer, uncovered, for about 1 hour, or until the sauce has thickened.

3 Cook the spaghetti in a large pan of rapidly boiling salted water for 10–12 minutes, or until *al dente*, then drain. Stir the parsley through the sauce and season with salt and pepper. Toss the sauce through the pasta and serve immediately.

Stir the meat constantly and break up any lumps with the back of a spoon.

Simmer the bolognese sauce uncovered until the liquid has reduced and the sauce has thickened.

NUTRITION PER SERVE
Protein 9 g; Fat 8 g; Carbohydrate 50 g; Dietary Fibre 7 g; Cholesterol 0 mg; 1695 kJ (405 Cal)

Lamb casserole with beans

PREPARATION TIME: 25 MINUTES + OVERNIGHT SOAKING | TOTAL COOKING TIME: 2 HOURS 15 MINUTES | SERVES 6

300 g (10½ oz/1½ cups) borlotti or red kidney beans
1 kg (2 lb 4 oz) boned leg of lamb
1 tablespoon olive oil
2 bacon slices, rind removed, chopped
1 large onion, chopped
2 garlic cloves, crushed
1 large carrot, chopped
500 ml (17 fl oz/2 cups) dry red wine
1 tablespoon tomato paste (concentrated purée)
375 ml (13 fl oz/1½ cups) beef stock
2 large rosemary sprigs
2 thyme sprigs

1 Put the beans in a bowl and cover with plenty of water. Leave to soak overnight, then drain well.

2 Preheat the oven to 160°C (315°F/Gas 2–3). Trim any fat from the lamb and cut into bite-sized cubes.

3 Heat the oil in a large ovenproof casserole dish and brown the lamb in two batches over high heat for 2 minutes. Remove all the lamb from the casserole dish and set aside.

4 Add the bacon and onion to the casserole dish. Cook over medium heat for 3 minutes, or until the onion is soft. Add the garlic and carrot and cook for 1 minute, or until aromatic.

5 Return the lamb and any juices to the dish, increase the heat to high and add the wine. Bring to the boil and cook for 2 minutes. Add the beans, tomato paste, stock and herbs, bring to the boil, cover and cook in the oven for 2 hours, or until the meat is tender. Stir occasionally. Skim off any fat from the surface and then season and remove the herb sprigs before serving.

NUTRITION PER SERVE
Protein 50 g; Fat 10 g; Carbohydrate 48 g; Dietary Fibre 9 g; Cholesterol 117 mg; 2367 kJ (565 Cal)

Remove the fat from the lamb then cut it into bite-sized cubes.

Return the meat and juices to the casserole dish, add the wine, and bring to the boil.

Chilli con carne

PREPARATION TIME: 25 MINUTES + OVERNIGHT SOAKING | TOTAL COOKING TIME: 2 HOURS 15 MINUTES | SERVES 6

185 g (6½ oz) dried black-eyed peas
650 g (1 lb 7 oz) tomatoes
1½ tablespoons oil
900 g (2 lb) trimmed chuck steak, cut into cubes
3 onions, thinly sliced
2 garlic cloves, chopped
2 teaspoons ground cumin
1 tablespoon paprika
½ teaspoon ground allspice
1–2 teaspoons chilli powder
1 tablespoon soft brown sugar
1 tablespoon red wine vinegar

1 Put the peas in a bowl, cover with plenty of water and leave overnight to soak. Drain well. Score a cross in the base of each tomato. Put the tomatoes in a bowl of boiling water for 30 seconds, then transfer to a bowl of cold water. Drain and peel the skin away from the cross. Halve the tomatoes and remove the seeds with a teaspoon. Chop the flesh finely.

2 Heat 1 tablespoon of the oil in a large heavy-based saucepan and add half the meat. Cook over medium–high heat for 2 minutes, or until well browned. Remove from the pan and repeat with the remaining meat, then remove from the pan.

3 Add the rest of the oil to the pan and add the onion. Cook over medium heat for 5 minutes, or until softened. Add the garlic and spices and cook, stirring, for 1 minute, or until aromatic. Add 500 ml (17 fl oz/2 cups) water and stir. Return the meat to the pan with the peas and tomato. Bring to the boil, then reduce the heat to low and simmer, partially covered, for 2 hours, or until the meat is tender and the chilli con carne is thick and dryish, stirring occasionally. Towards the end of the cooking time the mixture may start to catch, so add a little water if necessary. Stir through the sugar and vinegar, and season with salt to taste. Serve with flour tortillas, grated low-fat cheese and lime wedges.

NUTRITION PER SERVE
Protein 43 g; Fat 10 g; Carbohydrate 54 g; Dietary Fibre 10 g; Cholesterol 100 mg; 2040 kJ (486 Cal)

Soak the black-eyed peas in a bowl of water overnight before cooking them.

Drain the tomatoes then carefully peel the skin away from the cross.

Remove the tomato seeds with a teaspoon and then finely chop the flesh.

Bombay curry

PREPARATION TIME: 20 MINUTES | TOTAL COOKING TIME: 2 HOURS | SERVES 6

1 kg (2 lb 4 oz) chuck steak
1 tablespoon olive oil
2 onions, chopped
2 garlic cloves, crushed
2 green chillies, chopped
1 tablespoon grated fresh ginger
1½ teaspoons ground turmeric
1 teaspoon ground cumin
1 tablespoon ground coriander
½–1 teaspoon chilli powder
400 g (14 oz) tin tomatoes
250 ml (9 fl oz/1 cup) light coconut milk

1 Cut the beef into cubes. Heat the oil in a large saucepan and cook the onion until just soft.

2 Add the garlic, chilli, ginger, turmeric, cumin, coriander and chilli powder. Stir until heated; add the beef and cook, stirring, over high heat until well coated with the spice mixture.

3 Add 1 teaspoon salt and tomatoes. Simmer, covered, for 1–1½ hours, or until the beef is tender. Stir in the coconut milk and simmer, uncovered, for a further 5–10 minutes, or until slightly thickened.

NOTE: *Bombay curry is best made 1–2 days in advance to give the flavours time to develop. Store, covered, in the refrigerator.*

Add the garlic, chilli, ginger, turmeric, cumin, coriander and chilli powder.

Stir in the salt and tomatoes, then simmer, covered, until the meat is tender.

NUTRITION PER SERVE
Protein 35 g; Fat 15 g; Carbohydrate 5 g; Dietary Fibre 2 g; Cholesterol 120 mg; 1325 kJ (315 Cal)

Pork with pear and coriander salsa

PREPARATION TIME: 35 MINUTES | TOTAL COOKING TIME: 10 MINUTES | SERVES 4

3 beurre bosc pears
3–4 tablespoons lime juice
1 red onion, finely diced
2 large handfuls coriander (cilantro) leaves, finely chopped
½ teaspoon chilli flakes
1 teaspoon finely grated lime zest
cooking oil spray
4 pork steaks, butterflied

1 Cut the pears into quarters, remove the cores and chop into small dice. Sprinkle with the lime juice.

2 Combine the pear, onion, coriander, chilli flakes and lime zest and season.

3 Lightly spray a frying pan with oil and cook the pork steaks for 5 minutes on each side, or until cooked through. Serve with the salsa.

NOTE: *Use pears that are just ready to eat, not overripe or floury fruit.*

NUTRITION PER SERVE
Protein 24 g; Fat 7 g; Carbohydrate 17 g; Dietary Fibre 3 g; Cholesterol 53 mg; 930 kJ (234 Cal)

To dice an onion, slice it almost to the root, two or three times.

Then slice through vertically, leaving the root to hold it together. Then chop finely.

Cut the pears into quarters, then remove the cores and chop into dice.

Beef lasagne

PREPARATION TIME: 40 MINUTES | TOTAL COOKING TIME: 1 HOUR 35 MINUTES | SERVES 8

2 teaspoons olive oil
1 large onion, chopped
2 carrots, finely chopped
2 celery stalks, finely chopped
2 zucchini (courgettes), finely chopped
2 garlic cloves, crushed
500 g (1 lb 2 oz) lean minced (ground) beef
2 x 400 g (14 oz) tins chopped tomatoes
125 ml (4 fl oz/½ cup) beef stock
2 tablespoons tomato paste (concentrated purée)
2 teaspoons dried oregano
375 g (13 oz) lasagne sheets

CHEESE SAUCE

750 ml (26 fl oz/3 cups) skim milk
40 g (1½ oz/⅓ cup) cornflour (cornstarch)
100 g (3½ oz) reduced-fat cheddar cheese, grated

NUTRITION PER SERVE
Protein 15 g; Fat 12 g; Carbohydrate 50 g; Dietary Fibre 5 g; Cholesterol 10 mg; 1885 kJ (450 Cal)

1 Heat the olive oil in a large non-stick frying pan. Add the onion and cook until soft. Add the carrot, celery and zucchini and cook, stirring constantly, for about 5 minutes. Add the garlic and cook for another minute. Add the beef and cook over high heat, stirring, until well browned. Break up any lumps of meat.

2 Add the tomato, stock, tomato paste and oregano to the pan and stir to combine. Bring the mixture to the boil, then reduce the heat and simmer gently, partially covered, for 20 minutes, stirring occasionally.

3 Preheat the oven to 180°C (350°F/Gas 4). Spread a little of the meat sauce into the base of a 23 x 30 cm (9 x 12 inch) ovenproof dish. Arrange a layer of lasagne sheets in the dish.

4 Spread half the meat sauce over the top to cover evenly. Cover with another layer of lasagne sheets, a layer of meat sauce, then a final layer of lasagne sheets.

5 To make the cheese sauce, blend a little of the milk with the cornflour in a small saucepan, to form a smooth paste. Gradually blend in the remaining milk and stir constantly over low heat until the mixture boils and thickens. Remove from the heat and stir in the grated cheese until it has melted. Spread evenly over the top of the lasagne and bake for 1 hour.

6 Leave the lasagne to stand for 15 minutes before cutting into portions for serving.

When you add the meat, break up any lumps with a wooden spoon or fork.

Spread a little of the meat sauce over the base and cover evenly with lasagne sheets.

Spread the cheese sauce evenly over the top of the lasagne.

Beef with mango, raisin and fresh tomato salsa

PREPARATION TIME: 40 MINUTES | TOTAL COOKING TIME: 35 MINUTES | SERVES 4

2 tomatoes
1 mango
60 g (2¼ oz/½ cup) raisins
1 teaspoon tinned green peppercorns, drained and crushed
1 teaspoon finely grated lemon zest
2 tablespoons red wine vinegar
1 tablespoon olive oil
1 spring onion (scallion), shredded
750 g (1 lb 10 oz) piece eye fillet beef

1 Preheat the oven to 180°C (350°F/Gas 4). Score a cross in the base of each tomato. Place in a bowl of boiling water for 10 seconds, then plunge into cold water and peel the skin away from the cross. Scoop out the seeds and discard. Finely chop the tomato flesh and put in a bowl.

2 Peel and finely dice the mango and mix with the tomato and raisins. Mix together the peppercorns, lemon zest, vinegar and oil and add to the salsa. Season and scatter with spring onion.

3 Place the beef in a lightly oiled roasting tin and roast in the oven for 30–35 minutes. Leave to stand for 10 minutes before slicing.

NUTRITION PER SERVE
Protein 56 g; Fat 15 g; Carbohydrate 21 g; Dietary Fibre 3 g; Cholesterol 148 mg; 2000 kJ (500 Cal)

Score a cross in the base of each tomato to make it easier to peel off the skin.

Cut the cheeks from the mango, remove the skin and dice the flesh.

Mix the peppercorns, zest, vinegar and oil with the rest of the salsa ingredients.

Osso bucco with gremolata

PREPARATION TIME: 30 MINUTES | TOTAL COOKING TIME: 2 HOURS 40 MINUTES | SERVES 4

2 tablespoons olive oil
1 onion, finely chopped
1 garlic clove, crushed
1 kg (2 lb 4 oz) veal shin slices (osso bucco)
2 tablespoons plain (all-purpose) flour
410 g (14 oz) tin chopped tomatoes
250 ml (9 fl oz/1 cup) dry white wine
250 ml (9 fl oz/1 cup) chicken stock

GREMOLATA
2 tablespoons finely chopped fresh parsley
2 teaspoons grated lemon zest
1 teaspoon finely chopped garlic

1 Heat 1 tablespoon oil in a large shallow casserole dish. Add the onion and cook over low heat until soft and golden. Add the garlic. Cook for 1 minute, then remove from the dish.

2 Heat the remaining oil and brown the veal in batches, then remove. Return the onion to the casserole and stir in the flour. Cook for 30 seconds and remove from the heat. Slowly stir in the tomato, wine and stock, combining well with the flour. Return the veal to the casserole.

3 Return to the heat and bring to the boil, stirring. Cover and reduce the heat to low so that the casserole is just simmering. Cook for 2½ hours, or until the meat is very tender and almost falling off the bones.

4 To make the gremolata, combine the parsley, lemon zest and garlic in a bowl. Sprinkle over the osso bucco and serve with risotto or plain rice.

HINT: *Try to make this a day in advance to give the flavours time to develop and blend.*

NUTRITION PER SERVE
Protein 50 g; Fat 15 g; Carbohydrate 9.5 g; Dietary Fibre 2.5 g; Cholesterol 165 mg; 1700 kJ (405 Cal)

Heat the oil in the casserole and cook the veal pieces in batches until browned.

Make the traditional gremolata topping by mixing together the parsley, lemon zest and garlic.

Beef pot roast

PREPARATION TIME: 15 MINUTES | TOTAL COOKING TIME: 3 HOURS 15 MINUTES | SERVES 6

300 g (10½ oz) small pickling onions
2 carrots
3 parsnips, peeled
30 g (1 oz) butter
1–1.5 kg (2 lb 4 oz–3 lb 5 oz) piece of silverside, trimmed of fat (see NOTE)
3 tablespoons dry red wine
1 large tomato, finely chopped
250 ml (9 fl oz/1 cup) beef stock

1 Put the onions in a heatproof bowl and cover with boiling water. Leave for 1 minute, then drain well. Allow to cool and then peel off the skins.

2 Cut the carrots and parsnips in half lengthways then into even-sized pieces. Heat half the butter in a large heavy-based saucepan that will tightly fit the meat (it will shrink during cooking), add the onions, carrot and parsnip and cook, stirring, over medium–high heat until browned. Remove from the pan.

3 Add the remaining butter to the pan and add the meat, browning well all over. Increase the heat to high and pour in the wine. Bring to the boil, then add the tomato and stock. Return to the boil, then reduce the heat to low, cover and simmer for 2 hours, turning once. Add the vegetables and simmer, covered, for 1 hour.

4 Remove the meat from the pan and put it on a board ready for carving. Cover with foil and leave it to stand while you finish the sauce.

5 Increase the heat to high and boil the pan juices with the vegetables for 10 minutes to reduce and thicken slightly. Skim off any fat and taste before seasoning. Serve the meat and vegetables with the pan juices. Serve with mustard.

NUTRITION PER SERVE
Protein 60 g; Fat 10 g; Carbohydrate 95 g; Dietary Fibre 3.5 g; Cholesterol 185 mg; 1690 kJ (405 Cal)

NOTE: *Eye of silverside is a tender, long-shaped cut of silverside, which carves easily into serving-sized pieces. A regular piece of silverside or topside may be substituted.*

Put the pickling onions in a bowl and cover with boiling water.

Add the piece of meat to the pan and brown well on all sides.

Put the vegetables in with the meat, then cover and simmer for a further 1 hour.

Lamb cutlets with cannellini bean purée

PREPARATION TIME: 30 MINUTES + 1 HOUR REFRIGERATION | TOTAL COOKING TIME: 20 MINUTES | SERVES 4

8 lamb cutlets
4 garlic cloves
1 tablespoon chopped rosemary
2 teaspoons olive oil
2 x 400 g (14 oz) tins cannellini beans, drained
1 teaspoon ground cumin
125 ml (4 fl oz/½ cup) lemon juice
cooking oil spray
2 tablespoons balsamic vinegar

1 Trim the cutlets of excess fat from the outside edge and scrape the fat away from the bones. Place in a single layer in a shallow dish. Thinly slice 2 garlic cloves and mix with the rosemary, oil and ½ teaspoon salt and cracked black pepper. Pour over the meat, cover and refrigerate for 1 hour.

2 Rinse the beans and purée with the remaining garlic, the cumin and half the lemon juice in a food processor. Transfer to a saucepan, then set aside.

3 Lightly spray a non-stick frying pan with oil and cook the cutlets over medium heat for 1–2 minutes on each side. Add the vinegar and cook for 1 minute, turning to coat. Remove the cutlets and cover to keep warm. Add the remaining lemon juice to the pan and simmer for 2–3 minutes, or until the sauce thickens slightly. Warm the purée over medium heat and serve with the cutlets.

Peel 2 of the garlic cloves and thinly slice with a sharp knife.

Trim all the excess fat from the cutlets, and scrape any away from the bones.

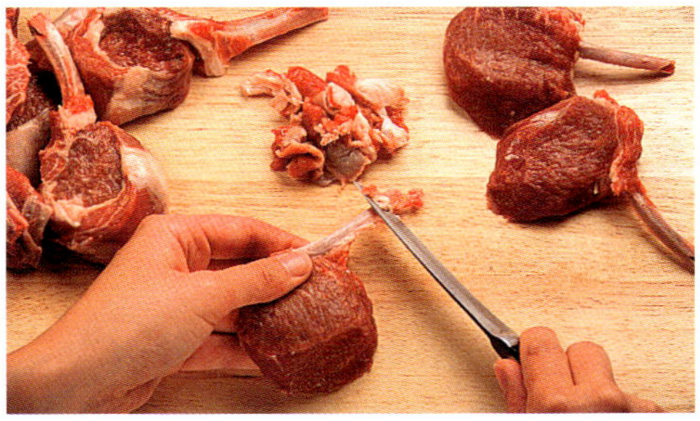

NUTRITION PER SERVE
Protein 30 g; Fat 8 g; Carbohydrate 45 g; Dietary Fibre 3.5 g; Cholesterol 50 mg; 1560 kJ (375 Cal)

Japanese pork and noodle stir-fry

PREPARATION TIME: 30 MINUTES | TOTAL COOKING TIME: 15 MINUTES | SERVES 4

1 tablespoon oil
150 g (5½ oz) pork loin, thinly sliced
5 spring onions (scallions), cut into short lengths
1 carrot, cut into thin strips
2 tablespoons Japanese soy sauce
200 g (7 oz) Chinese cabbage, shredded
500 g (1 lb 2 oz) hokkien (egg) noodles, gently pulled apart to separate
1 tablespoon worcestershire sauce
1 tablespoon mirin
2 teaspoons caster (superfine) sugar
90 g (3¼ oz/1 cup) bean sprouts, trimmed
1 sheet toasted nori (dried seaweed), shredded

1 Heat the oil in a large wok over medium heat. Stir-fry the pork, spring onion and carrot for 1–2 minutes, or until the pork just changes colour.

2 Add the soy sauce, cabbage, noodles, worcestershire sauce, mirin, sugar and 2 tablespoons water. Cover and cook for 1 minute.

3 Add the bean sprouts and toss well to coat the vegetables and noodles in the sauce. Serve immediately, sprinkled with the shredded nori.

NUTRITION PER SERVE
Protein 25 g; Fat 8 g; Carbohydrate 93 g; Dietary Fibre 5.5 g; Cholesterol 40 mg; 2300 kJ (550 Cal)

Finely shred the Chinese cabbage with a large, sharp knife.

Use your fingers to remove the straggly ends from the bean sprouts.

Stir-fry the pork, spring onion and carrot until the pork just changes colour.

Pork rolls with roasted capsicum

PREPARATION TIME: 40 MINUTES | TOTAL COOKING TIME: 30 MINUTES | SERVES 4

SAUCE
185 ml (6 fl oz/¾ cup) beef stock
2 teaspoons soy sauce
2 tablespoons dry red wine
2 teaspoons wholegrain mustard
2 teaspoons cornflour (cornstarch)

1 red capsicum (pepper)
4 x 150 g (5½ oz) lean pork leg steaks
90 g (3¼ oz/⅓ cup) ricotta cheese
2 spring onions (scallions), finely chopped
1 garlic clove, crushed
70 g (2½ oz) rocket (arugula)
4 small lean slices prosciutto (about 35 g/1¼ oz)
cooking oil spray

NUTRITION PER SERVE
Protein 40 g; Fat 5 g; Carbohydrate 3.5 g; Dietary Fibre 1 g; Cholesterol 95 mg; 925 kJ (220 Cal)

1 To make the sauce, put the beef stock, soy sauce, red wine and mustard in a saucepan. Blend the cornflour with 1 tablespoon water and add to the pan. Stir until the mixture boils.

2 Cut the capsicum into quarters and remove the seeds and membrane. Grill (broil) until the skin blisters and blackens. Cool under a damp tea towel (dish towel), peel and cut the flesh into thin strips.

3 Flatten each steak into a thin square between two sheets of plastic, using a rolling pin or mallet. Combine the ricotta, spring onion and garlic in a bowl, then spread evenly over the pork. Top with a layer of rocket and prosciutto. Place a quarter of the capsicum at one end and roll up to enclose the capsicum. Tie with string or secure with toothpicks at even intervals.

4 Spray a non-stick frying pan with oil and fry the pork rolls over medium heat for 5 minutes, or until well browned. Add the sauce to the pan and simmer over low heat for 10–15 minutes, or until the rolls are cooked. Remove the string or toothpicks. Slice and serve with the sauce.

Flatten the pork between two pieces of plastic wrap, using a rolling pin or mallet.

Secure the pork rolls with string or toothpicks at even intervals.

Add the sauce to the pan and simmer over low heat until cooked through.

Beef stroganoff

PREPARATION TIME: 20 MINUTES | TOTAL COOKING TIME: 25 MINUTES | SERVES 4

500 g (1 lb 2 oz) rump steak
cooking oil spray
1 onion, sliced
¼ teaspoon paprika
250 g (9 oz) button mushrooms, halved
2 tablespoons tomato paste (concentrated purée)
125 ml (4 fl oz/½ cup) beef stock
125 ml (4 fl oz/½ cup) low-fat evaporated milk
3 teaspoons cornflour (cornstarch)
3 tablespoons chopped parsley

1 Remove any excess fat from the steak and slice into thin strips. Cook in batches in a large, lightly greased non-stick frying pan over high heat, until just cooked. Remove from the pan.

2 Lightly spray the pan and cook the onion, paprika and mushrooms over medium heat until the onion has softened. Add the meat, tomato paste, stock and 125 ml (4 fl oz/½ cup) water. Bring to the boil, then reduce the heat and simmer for 10 minutes.

3 In a small bowl, mix the evaporated milk with the cornflour. Add to the pan and stir until the sauce boils and thickens. Sprinkle with parsley.

NUTRITION PER SERVE
Protein 35 g; Fat 4 g; Carbohydrate 8 g; Dietary Fibre 2.5 g; Cholesterol 85 mg; 900 kJ (215 Cal)

Slice the rump steak into thin strips after removing any excess fat.

Stir the onion, paprika and mushrooms until the onion has softened.

Stir the evaporated milk into the cornflour until the mixture is smooth.

Mediterranean lamb casserole

PREPARATION TIME: 15 MINUTES | TOTAL COOKING TIME: 1 HOUR | SERVES 4

1 tablespoon olive oil
750 g (1 lb 10 oz) lamb from the bone, diced
1 large onion, sliced
2 garlic cloves, crushed
2 carrots, chopped
2 parsnips, chopped
400 g (14 oz) tin chopped tomatoes
2 tablespoons tomato paste
(concentrated purée)
2 teaspoons chopped rosemary
125 ml (4 fl oz/½ cup) dry red wine
250 ml (9 fl oz/1 cup) chicken stock

1 Heat the oil in a large saucepan and cook the lamb, in batches, for 3–4 minutes, or until browned. Remove from the pan and keep warm. Add the onion and garlic to the pan and cook for 2–3 minutes, or until the onion is soft.

2 Return the lamb and juices to the pan. Add the carrot, parsnip, tomato, tomato paste, rosemary, wine and stock and bring to the boil. Reduce the heat and cover the pan. Simmer the casserole for 50 minutes, or until the lamb is tender and the sauce has thickened. Serve with soft polenta or couscous.

Add the onion and garlic to the pan and cook until the onion is soft.

Simmer until the lamb is tender and the sauce has thickened.

NUTRITION PER SERVE
Protein 45 g; Fat 12 g; Carbohydrate 12 g; Dietary Fibre 4.5 g; Cholesterol 125 mg; 1517 kJ (362 Cal)

Veal, lemon and caper stew

PREPARATION TIME: 30 MINUTES | TOTAL COOKING TIME: 2 HOURS | SERVES 6

1 tablespoon olive oil
50 g (1¾ oz) butter
1 kg (2 lb 4 oz) stewing veal, cut into 4 cm (1½ inch) chunks
300 g (10½ oz) French shallots (eschalots)
3 leeks, white part only, cut into large cubes
2 garlic cloves, crushed
1 tablespoon plain (all-purpose) flour
500 ml (17 fl oz/2 cups) chicken stock
1 teaspoon grated lemon zest
4 tablespoons lemon juice
2 bay leaves
2 tablespoons capers, drained and well rinsed

NUTRITION PER SERVE
Protein 40 g; Fat 13 g; Carbohydrate 5 g; Dietary Fibre 2 g; Cholesterol 160 mg; 1300 kJ (300 Cal)

1 Preheat the oven to 180°C (350°F/Gas 4). Heat the oil and half the butter in a large, heavy-based saucepan. Brown the veal in batches over medium–high heat and transfer to a large casserole dish.

2 Blanch the shallots in boiling water for 30 seconds, then peel and add to the saucepan with the leeks. Gently cook for 5 minutes, or until soft and golden. Add the garlic, cook for 1 minute, then transfer to the casserole dish.

3 Melt the remaining butter in the pan, add the flour and cook for 30 seconds. Remove from the heat, add the stock and stir until well combined. Return to the heat and cook, stirring, until the sauce begins to bubble.

4 Pour the sauce into the casserole dish and stir in the lemon zest, lemon juice and bay leaves. Cover and bake for 1–1½ hours, or until the veal is tender. During the last 20 minutes of cooking, remove the lid to allow the sauces to reduce a little. Stir in the capers and season with salt and pepper before serving.

Add the leeks and peeled shallots to the pan and gently fry until soft and golden.

Remove the pan from the heat and stir in the stock, scraping up the brown bits.

Pasta all'arrabbiata

PREPARATION TIME: 20 MINUTES | TOTAL COOKING TIME: 1 HOUR | SERVES 4

4 double-smoked bacon slices, rind removed
2 teaspoons olive oil
4 red chillies, seeded and chopped
2 large onions, finely chopped
3 garlic cloves, crushed
800 g (1 lb 12 oz) very ripe tomatoes, finely chopped
500 g (1 lb 2 oz) lasagnette pasta
2 tablespoons chopped parsley
grated parmesan cheese, to serve

1 Chop the bacon. Heat the olive oil in a heavy-based saucepan and add the bacon, chilli, onion and garlic. Cook over medium heat for about 8 minutes, stirring occasionally.

2 Add the tomato and 3 tablespoons water to the pan and season to taste with salt and pepper. Cover and simmer for about 40 minutes, or until the sauce is thick and rich.

3 Cook the pasta in a large saucepan of rapidly boiling water until *al dente*. Drain and rinse thoroughly in a colander, then return the pasta to the pan and keep warm.

4 Add the parsley to the sauce and season again if necessary. Pour the sauce over the pasta, tossing to coat the pasta thoroughly. Serve sprinkled with a little grated parmesan.

NOTE: *Good-quality bacon and very ripe, red, full-flavoured tomatoes are essential to the flavour of this dish.*

Simmer the tomato sauce until it becomes rich and thick.

Toss the pasta and sauce together with two wooden spoons.

NUTRITION PER SERVE
Protein 30 g; Fat 12 g; Carbohydrate 95 g; Dietary Fibre 10 g; Cholesterol 30 mg; 2765 kJ (600 Cal)

Tagine of lamb with quince and lemon

PREPARATION TIME: 25 MINUTES | TOTAL COOKING TIME: 2 HOURS 10 MINUTES | SERVES 4

1.5 kg (3 lb 5 oz) boned shoulder of lamb, cut into 12 even pieces
1 onion, finely chopped
2 garlic cloves, crushed
1 cinnamon stick
1 teaspoon ground ginger
½ teaspoon saffron threads
1 large quince, peeled, seeded and cut into 12 pieces (see HINT)
90 g (3¼ oz/¼ cup) honey
1 teaspoon ground cinnamon
½ preserved lemon

1 Trim the lamb of excess fat and place in a large saucepan. Add the onion, garlic, cinnamon stick, ginger and saffron and enough cold water to cover. Slowly bring to the boil, stirring occasionally. Reduce the heat, cover and simmer for 45 minutes. Transfer the meat to a casserole dish.

2 Add the quince, honey and ground cinnamon to the cooking liquid and simmer for 15 minutes, or until the quince is tender. Discard the cinnamon, remove the quince and add to the meat, reserving the liquid.

3 Preheat the oven to 180°C (350°F/Gas 4). Boil the cooking liquid for 30 minutes, or until reduced by half, then pour over the meat and quince. Remove and discard the flesh from the preserved lemon. Slice the zest thinly, then add to the meat. Cover and bake for 40 minutes, or until the meat is tender.

HINT: *As you work, place the peeled quince in water with a little lemon juice to prevent discolouring.*

Add the onion, garlic, cinnamon stick, ginger, saffron and cold water to the lamb.

Add the quince, honey and ground cinnamon to the cooking liquid.

NUTRITION PER SERVE
Protein 80 g; Fat 15 g; Carbohydrate 20 g; Dietary Fibre 3 g; Cholesterol 250 mg; 2160 kJ (515 Cal)

Chicken

Curried chicken in spicy tomato sauce

PREPARATION TIME: 35 MINUTES | TOTAL COOKING TIME: 1 HOUR 40 MINUTES | SERVES 10

1 tablespoon olive oil
2 x 1.5 kg (3 lb 5 oz) chickens, jointed
1 onion, sliced
½ teaspoon ground cloves
1 teaspoon ground turmeric
2 teaspoons garam masala
3 teaspoons chilli powder
3 garlic cloves
1 tablespoon finely chopped fresh ginger
1 tablespoon poppy seeds
2 teaspoons fennel seeds
3 cardamom pods, seeds removed (see NOTE)
250 ml (9 fl oz/1 cup) light coconut milk
1 star anise
1 cinnamon stick
4 large tomatoes, roughly chopped
2 tablespoons lime juice

NUTRITION PER SERVE
Protein 35 g; Fat 11 g; Carbohydrate 6.5 g; Dietary Fibre 1.5 g; Cholesterol 75 mg; 1027 kJ (245 Cal)

1 Heat the olive oil in a large frying pan, add the chicken in batches and cook for 5–10 minutes, or until browned, then transfer to a large saucepan.

2 Add the onion to the frying pan and cook, stirring, for 10–12 minutes, or until golden. Stir in the ground cloves, turmeric, garam masala and chilli powder, and cook, stirring, for 1 minute, then add to the chicken.

3 Place the garlic, ginger, poppy seeds, fennel seeds, cardamom seeds and 2 tablespoons of the coconut milk in a food processor or blender, and process until smooth. Add the spice mixture, remaining coconut milk, star anise, cinnamon, tomato and 3 tablespoons water to the chicken.

4 Simmer, covered, for 45 minutes, or until the chicken is tender. Remove the chicken, cover and keep warm. Bring the cooking liquid to the boil and boil for 20–25 minutes, or until reduced by half. Mix the lime juice with the cooking liquid and pour over the chicken. Serve with low-fat yoghurt.

NOTE: *To remove the cardamom seeds from the cardamom pods, crush the pods with the flat side of a heavy knife, then peel away the pod with your fingers, scraping out the seeds.*

Crush the cardamom pods with the back of a knife and then remove the seeds.

Brown the chicken for 5–10 minutes, a few pieces at a time.

Process the garlic, spices and coconut milk until the mixture is smooth.

Lime steamed chicken

PREPARATION TIME: 15 MINUTES | TOTAL COOKING TIME: 15 MINUTES | SERVES 4

2 limes, thinly sliced
4 boneless, skinless chicken breasts
500 g (1 lb 2 oz/1 bunch) bok choy (pak choy)
500 g (1 lb 2 oz/1 bunch) choy sum
1 teaspoon sesame oil
1 tablespoon peanut oil
125 ml (4 fl oz/½ cup) oyster sauce
4 tablespoons lime juice

1 Line the base of a bamboo steamer with the lime, place the chicken on top and season. Place over a wok with a little water in the base, cover and steam for 8–10 minutes, or until the chicken is cooked through. Cover the chicken and keep warm. Remove the water from the wok.

2 Wash and trim the greens. Heat the oils in the wok and cook the greens for 2–3 minutes, or until just wilted.

3 Combine the oyster sauce and lime juice and pour over the greens when they are cooked. Place the chicken on serving plates on top of the greens and serve with rice, and lime slices.

NOTE: *The Asian green vegetables used in this recipe, bok choy and choy sum, can be replaced by any green vegetables, such as broccoli, snow peas (mangetouts) or English spinach.*

NUTRITION PER SERVE
Protein 43 g; Fat 8.9 g; Carbohydrate 11.5 g; Dietary Fibre 2.8 g; Cholesterol 117 mg; 1297 kJ (310 Cal)

Lay the lime slices in the bamboo steamer, put the chicken on top and steam until cooked.

Heat the oils in the wok and stir-fry the greens until they are wilted.

Mix together the oyster sauce and lime juice and pour over the cooked greens.

Chicken with tomatoes, olives and capers

PREPARATION TIME: 20 MINUTES | TOTAL COOKING TIME: 1 HOUR | SERVES 4

2 tablespoons olive oil
1 red onion, cut into thin wedges
1 celery stalk, sliced
150 g (5½ oz) cap mushrooms, sliced
3–4 garlic cloves, thinly sliced
8 boneless, skinless chicken thighs
plain (all-purpose) flour, for dusting
125 ml (4 fl oz/½ cup) dry white wine
300 ml (10½ fl oz) chicken stock
400 g (14 oz) tin chopped tomatoes
1 tablespoon tomato paste (concentrated purée)
60 g (2¼ oz/⅓ cup) black olives
1 tablespoon capers, drained and well rinsed

1 Heat half the oil in a large non-stick frying pan. Add the onion, celery, mushrooms and garlic and cook, stirring, for 5 minutes, or until the onion is soft. Remove from the pan.

2 Coat the chicken lightly in flour, shaking off any excess. Heat the remaining oil in the frying pan and cook the chicken, in batches, turning once, for 5 minutes, or until well browned. Add the wine and stock and cook for a further 2 minutes.

3 Return the vegetables to the pan and add the tomato and tomato paste. Simmer, partially covered, for 40 minutes, or until thickened. Add the olives and capers and season.

Cook the onion, celery, mushrooms and garlic in a frying pan.

Cook the chicken, turning once, until it is well browned all over.

NUTRITION PER SERVE
Protein 11 g; Fat 11 g; Carbohydrate 11 g; Dietary Fibre 4.3 g; Cholesterol 14 mg; 874 kJ (210 Cal)

Steamed lemongrass and ginger chicken

PREPARATION TIME: 25 MINUTES | TOTAL COOKING TIME: 40 MINUTES | SERVES 4

200 g (7 oz) fresh egg noodles
4 boneless, skinless chicken breasts
2 lemongrass stems
5 cm (2 inch) piece fresh ginger, cut into thin strips
1 lime, thinly sliced
500 ml (17 fl oz/2 cups) chicken stock
350 g (12 oz/1 bunch) choy sum, cut into 10 cm (4 inch) lengths
800 g (1 lb 12 oz) Chinese broccoli, cut into 10 cm (4 inch) lengths
3 tablespoons kecap manis (see NOTE, page 13)
3 tablespoons soy sauce
1 teaspoon sesame oil
toasted sesame seeds, to garnish

1 Cook the egg noodles in a saucepan of boiling water for 5 minutes, then drain and keep warm.

2 Cut each chicken breast fillet horizontally through the middle so that you are left with eight thin flat chicken fillets.

3 Cut the lemongrass into lengths that are about 5 cm (2 inches) longer than the chicken breasts, then cut in half lengthways. Place one piece of lemongrass onto one half of each chicken breast, top with some ginger and lime slices, then top with the other half of the breast.

4 Pour the stock into a wok and bring to a simmer. Place two of the chicken breasts in a paper-lined bamboo steamer. Place the steamer over the wok and steam over the simmering stock for 12–15 minutes, or until the chicken is tender. Remove the chicken from the steamer, cover and keep warm. Repeat with the other breasts.

5 Steam the greens in the same way for 3 minutes, or until tender. Bring the stock in the wok to the boil.

6 Place the kecap manis, soy sauce and sesame oil in a bowl and whisk together well.

7 Divide the noodles among four serving plates and ladle the boiling stock over them Top with a pile of Asian greens, then add the chicken and generously drizzle each serve with the sauce. Sprinkle with toasted sesame seeds and serve.

NUTRITION PER SERVE
Protein 65 g; Fat 7.5 g; Carbohydrate 37 g; Dietary Fibre 9 g; Cholesterol 119 mg; 2045 kJ (488 Cal)

Cut each chicken breast in half horizontally through the middle.

Top the bottom half of each fillet with lemongrass, ginger and lime.

Steam the lemongrass ch cken breasts until cooked and tender.

Baked chicken and leek risotto

PREPARATION TIME: 10 MINUTES | TOTAL COOKING TIME: 40 MINUTES | SERVES 6

1 tablespoon oil
1 leek, white part only, thinly sliced
2 boneless, skinless chicken breasts, cubed
440 g (15½ oz/2 cups) arborio rice
3 tablespoons dry white wine
1.25 litres (44 fl oz/5 cups) chicken stock
35 g (1¼ oz/⅓ cup) grated parmesan cheese
2 tablespoons thyme leaves
thyme leaves and parmesan cheese, for serving

1 Preheat the oven to 150°C (300°F/Gas 2) and place a 5 litre (175 fl oz/20 cup) ovenproof dish with a lid in the oven to warm. Heat the oil in a saucepan over medium heat, add the leek and cook for 2 minutes, or until soft.

2 Add the chicken and cook, stirring, for 2–3 minutes, or until it colours. Add the rice and stir so that it is well coated. Cook for 1 minute.

3 Add the wine and stock and bring to the boil. Pour the mixture into the warm ovenproof dish and cover. Place in the oven and cook for 30 minutes, stirring halfway through. Remove from the oven and stir through the parmesan and thyme leaves. Season to taste. Sprinkle with extra thyme leaves and a little parmesan and serve.

NUTRITION PER SERVE
Protein 28 g; Fat 15 g; Carbohydrate 60 g; Dietary Fibre 3 g; Cholesterol 75 mg; 2014 kJ (480 Cal)

Cook the leek for a couple of minutes over medium heat until it is soft.

Add the arborio rice to the pan and stir until it is well coated.

Cook the risotto in the oven for 30 minutes, then remove and stir in the parmesan and thyme.

Spicy chicken patties

PREPARATION TIME: 10 MINUTES + 20 MINUTES REFRIGERATION | TOTAL COOKING TIME: 10 MINUTES | SERVES 4

500 g (1 lb 2 oz) minced (ground) chicken
4 spring onions (scallions), finely chopped
2 large handfuls coriander (cilantro) leaves, finely chopped
2 garlic cloves, crushed
¾ teaspoon cayenne pepper
1 egg white, lightly beaten
1 tablespoon oil
1 lemon, halved

1 Preheat the oven to 170°C (325°F/Gas 3). Mix together all the ingredients except the oil and lemon, season with salt and pepper and shape the mixture into 4 patties. Refrigerate for 20 minutes before cooking.

2 Heat the oil in a large frying pan over medium heat, add the patties and cook for about 5 minutes on each side, or until browned and cooked through.

3 Squeeze the lemon on the cooked patties and drain well on paper towels. Serve with a salad or use to make burgers with crusty rolls.

NUTRITION PER SERVE
Protein 25 g; Fat 12 g; Carbohydrate 1 g; Dietary Fibre 1 g; Cholesterol 105 mg; 895 kJ (215 Cal)

Mix together all the ingredients and then shape into patties.

Cook the patties for about 5 minutes on each side, or until cooked through.

Squeeze the lemon over the patties and drain on paper towels before serving.

Chicken pies

PREPARATION TIME: 50 MINUTES + 30 MINUTES REFRIGERATION | TOTAL COOKING TIME: 1 HOUR | SERVES 4

300 g (10½ oz) boneless, skinless chicken breast
1 bay leaf
500 ml (17 fl oz/2 cups) chicken stock
2 large potatoes, peeled and chopped
250 g (9 oz) orange sweet potato, peeled and chopped
2 celery stalks, chopped
2 carrots, chopped
1 onion, chopped
1 parsnip, chopped
1 garlic clove, crushed
1 tablespoon cornflour (cornstarch)
250 ml (9 fl oz/1 cup) skim milk
155 g (5½ oz/1 cup) frozen peas, thawed
1 tablespoon snipped chives
1 tablespoon chopped parsley
185 g (6½ oz/1½ cups) self-raising flour
20 g (¾ oz) butter
4 tablespoons milk
1 egg, lightly beaten
2 teaspoons sesame seeds

NUTRITION PER SERVE
Protein 30 g; Fat 10 g; Carbohydrate 65 g; Dietary Fibre 9.5 g; Cholesterol 100 mg; 2045 kJ (490 Cal)

1 Combine the chicken, bay leaf and stock in a large, deep non-stick frying pan and simmer for about 10 minutes. Remove the chicken and set aside. When cool, cut into small pieces. Add the potato, sweet potato, celery and carrot and simmer, covered, for about 10 minutes. Remove the vegetables from the pan. Add the onion, parsnip and garlic to the pan and simmer for about 10 minutes. Discard the bay leaf. Purée in a food processor until smooth.

2 Stir the cornflour into 2 tablespoons of the skim milk until it forms a smooth paste, stir into the mixture with the remaining milk and then return to the pan. Stir over low heat until the mixture boils and thickens. Preheat the oven to 200°C (400°F/Gas 6). Combine the mixture with the remaining vegetables, chicken and herbs. Season with salt and pepper. Spoon into four 435 ml (15¼ fl oz/1¾ cup) capacity ramekins.

3 To make the pastry, sift the flour into a bowl, rub in the butter with your fingertips, then make a well in the centre. Combine the milk with 4 tablespoons water and add enough to make a soft dough. Turn out onto a lightly floured surface and knead. Cut the dough into four portions and roll each out so that it is 1 cm (½ inch) larger than the top of the ramekin. Brush the edge of the dough with some of the egg and fit over the top of each ramekin, pressing the edge firmly to seal. Brush the pastry tops with beaten egg and sprinkle with the sesame seeds. Bake for about 30 minutes, until the tops are golden.

Purée the cooked onion, parsnip and garlic together until smooth.

Add enough liquid to the dry ingredients to make a soft dough.

Brush the edge of the dough with egg, then press over the top of each ramekin.

Lemon chilli chicken

PREPARATION TIME: 20 MINUTES | TOTAL COOKING TIME: 35 MINUTES | SERVES 4

2 garlic cloves, chopped
1 tablespoon grated fresh ginger
2 tablespoons olive oil
600 g (1 lb 5 oz) boneless, skinless chicken thighs
1 teaspoon ground coriander
2 teaspoons ground cumin
½ teaspoon ground turmeric
1 red chilli, chopped
125 ml (4 fl oz/½ cup) lemon juice
185 ml (6 fl oz/¾ cup) dry white wine
3 large handfuls coriander (cilantro) leaves

1 Blend the garlic, ginger and 1 tablespoon water into a paste in a small food processor or with a mortar and pestle. Heat the olive oil in a heavy-based frying pan and brown the chicken in batches. Remove and set aside.

2 Add the garlic paste to the pan and cook, stirring, for 1 minute. Add the coriander, cumin, turmeric and chilli and stir-fry for 1 minute more. Stir in the lemon juice and wine.

3 Add the chicken pieces to the pan. Bring to the boil, reduce the heat, cover and cook for 20–25 minutes, stirring occasionally, until the chicken is tender. Uncover and cook the sauce over high heat for 5 minutes to reduce it by half. Stir in the fresh coriander and season to taste. Serve with rice.

Brown the chicken in batches to stop the meat from stewing.

Add the coriander, cumin, turmeric and chilli and stir-fry for 1 minute.

NUTRITION PER SERVE
Protein 30 g; Fat 15 g; Carbohydrate 0 g; Dietary Fibre 0 g; Cholesterol 105 mg; 1290 kJ (310 Cal)

Chicken with black bean sauce

PREPARATION TIME: 10 MINUTES | TOTAL COOKING TIME: 20 MINUTES | SERVES 4

2 tablespoons black beans
1 tablespoon oil
1 small onion, finely chopped
1 tablespoon finely chopped fresh ginger
1 garlic clove, finely chopped
1 red chilli, seeded and finely chopped
310 ml (10¾ fl oz/1¼ cups) chicken stock
2 teaspoons cornflour (cornstarch)
2 teaspoons sesame oil
4 boneless, skinless chicken breasts

1 Rinse the black beans under cold water for 3–4 minutes to remove any excess saltiness. Drain well.

2 Heat the oil in a small saucepan and add the onion, ginger, garlic and chilli. Cook over low heat until the onion is soft but not browned. Add the chicken stock and bring to the boil. Reduce the heat and simmer for 5 minutes.

3 Mix the cornflour and 1 tablespoon water in a small bowl and add to the pan. Keep stirring and the mixture will thicken. Allow to simmer for 3 minutes, then add the beans and sesame oil and mix together well.

4 Grill (broil) the chicken under a preheated grill (broiler) for 5 minutes on each side, or until cooked through and tender. Serve with the sauce.

NOTE: *Black beans are available tinned or in vacuum packs from Asian food stores. Do not confuse these Chinese black beans with Mexican black turtle beans that are available from health food shops. The two varieties are very different.*

Rinse the black beans under running water to get rid of excess saltiness.

Cook until the onion is soft but not browned, then add the stock.

NUTRITION PER SERVE
Protein 26 g; Fat 3.5 g; Carbohydrate 2 g; Dietary Fibre 0 g; Cholesterol 55 mg; 580 kJ (140 Cal)

Chicken with coriander chutney and spiced eggplant

PREPARATION TIME: 1 HOUR 10 MINUTES + OVERNIGHT REFRIGERATION + 30 MINUTES SOAKING | TOTAL COOKING TIME: 1 HOUR 10 MINUTES | SERVES 4

250 g (9 oz/1 cup) low-fat plain yoghurt
1 tablespoon lemon juice
½ onion, roughly chopped
2 garlic cloves, finely chopped
2 teaspoons grated fresh ginger
½ teaspoon ground cumin
750 g (1 lb 10 oz) boneless, skinless chicken thighs, trimmed of fat, cut into large cubes
cooking oil spray
4 pieces naan bread
low-fat natural yoghurt, to serve

SPICED EGGPLANT

1 large eggplant (aubergine)
1 tablespoon oil
1 onion, finely chopped
3 teaspoons finely chopped fresh ginger
2 garlic cloves, crushed
½ teaspoon ground turmeric
1 teaspoon ground cumin
1 tomato, finely diced
2 teaspoons lemon juice

CORIANDER CHUTNEY

3 tablespoons lemon juice
100 g (3½ oz/1 bunch) coriander (cilantro) leaves and stems, roughly chopped
½ onion, finely chopped
1 tablespoon finely chopped fresh ginger
½ jalapeño chilli (pepper), seeded and diced
1 teaspoon sugar

1 Combine the yoghurt, lemon juice, onion, garlic, ginger and cumin in a large non-metallic bowl, add the chicken and toss. Cover and refrigerate overnight.

2 Preheat the oven to 240°C (475°F/Gas 8). Soak eight wooden skewers in water for 30 minutes. Prick the eggplant a few times, put on a baking tray and bake for 35–40 minutes. Cool. Reduce the oven to 200°C (400°F/Gas 6).

3 To make the chutney, put the lemon juice, coriander and 3 tablespoons water in a food processor and process until smooth. Add the remaining ingredients and season.

4 Cut the eggplant in half, scoop out the flesh and coarsely chop. Heat the oil in a frying pan. Add the onion and cook for 5 minutes. Add the ginger and garlic and cook for 2 minutes. Add the spices and cook for 1 minute, then add the tomato and 3 tablespoons water and simmer for 5 minutes. Stir in the eggplant and lemon juice and season. Cook for 2 minutes, then remove from the heat and keep warm. Thread the chicken onto skewers. Lightly spray a chargrill pan with oil and cook over medium heat for 4–6 minutes each side. Heat the naan in the oven. Put on a plate and spread some eggplant in the centre. Lay two chicken skewers on top and drizzle with chutney and yoghurt.

NUTRITION PER SERVE
Protein 50 g; Fat 15 g; Carbohydrate 26 g; Dietary Fibre 5.5 g; Cholesterol 105 mg; 1956 kJ (467 Cal)

Roast the eggplant on a baking tray until very soft and wrinkled.

Process the lemon juice, coriander and water until you have a smooth paste.

Chargrill the chicken skewers until they are tender and cooked through.

Chicken with peach, red capsicum and ginger salsa

PREPARATION TIME: 20 MINUTES | TOTAL COOKING TIME: 10 MINUTES | SERVES 4

cooking oil spray
4 boneless, skinless chicken breasts
3 tablespoons white wine vinegar
2 tablespoons caster (superfine) sugar
2 teaspoons grated fresh ginger
1 garlic clove, crushed
½ teaspoon ground cumin
1 large handful coriander (cilantro) leaves, chopped
1 large handful mint, chopped
1 red capsicum (pepper), diced
1 small red onion, finely diced
1 small red chilli, finely chopped
3 peaches, tinned or fresh, diced

1 Lightly spray a chargrill pan with oil and cook the chicken breasts for 5 minutes on each side or until tender and cooked through.

2 Combine the vinegar, sugar, ginger, garlic, cumin, coriander and mint.

3 Put the capsicum, onion, chilli and peaches in a large bowl. Gently stir through the vinegar herb mixture and serve at once with the chicken.

NUTRITION PER SERVE
Protein 27 g; Fat 2.5 g; Carbohydrate 24 g; Dietary Fibre 3 g; Cholesterol 55 mg; 960 kJ (240 Cal)

Use fresh peaches if they are in season, otherwise tinned can be used.

Mix together the vinegar, sugar, ginger, garlic, cumin, coriander and mint.

Stir through the vinegar herb mixture and serve the salsa with the chicken at once.

Chicken stew with white beans and zucchini

PREPARATION TIME: 15 MINUTES | TOTAL COOKING TIME: 1 HOUR | SERVES 4

- 1 tablespoon olive oil
- 8 boneless, skinless chicken thighs
- 1 onion, halved and thinly sliced
- 4 garlic cloves, finely chopped
- 3 tablespoons dry white wine
- 250 ml (9 fl oz/1 cup) chicken stock
- 1 tablespoon finely chopped rosemary
- 1 teaspoon grated lemon zest
- 1 bay leaf
- 2 x 400 g (14 oz) tins cannellini beans, drained and rinsed
- 3 zucchini (courgettes), halved lengthways, cut on the diagonal

1 Heat the oil in a large ovenproof casserole dish. Add the chicken in batches, and cook for 4 minutes on each side, or until browned. Remove.

2 Add the onion to the dish and cook for 5 minutes, or until soft. Add the garlic and cook for 1 minute, or until fragrant, then add the wine and chicken stock and bring to the boil, scraping the bottom of the pan to remove any sediment.

3 Return the chicken and any juices to the pan along with the rosemary, lemon zest and bay leaf. Reduce the heat and simmer, covered, for 40 minutes, or until the chicken is tender. Stir in the cannellini beans and zucchini and cook for 5 minutes more, or until the zucchini is tender.

STORAGE TIME: *Can be frozen in snap-lock bags or an airtight container for up to 3 months.*

Brown the chicken thigh cutlets in batches in a large casserole dish.

Stir in the drained and rinsed cannellini beans and the zucchini and cook for 5 minutes more.

NUTRITION PER SERVE

Protein 37 g; Fat 8 g; Carbohydrate 25 g; Dietary Fibre 15 g; Cholesterol 50 mg; 1394 kJ (334 Cal)

Asian barbecued chicken

PREPARATION TIME: 10 MINUTES + 2 HOURS MARINATING | TOTAL COOKING TIME: 25 MINUTES | SERVES 6

2 garlic cloves, finely chopped
3 tablespoons hoisin sauce
3 teaspoons light soy sauce
3 teaspoons honey
1 teaspoon sesame oil
2 tablespoons tomato sauce (ketchup) or sweet chilli sauce
2 spring onions (scallions), finely sliced
1.5 kg (3 lb 5 oz) chicken wings

NUTRITION PER SERVE
Protein 26 g; Fat 8.5 g; Carbohydrate 9 g; Dietary Fibre 1.5 g; Cholesterol 111 mg; 916 kJ (219 Cal)

1 To make the marinade, combine the garlic, hoisin sauce, soy sauce, honey, sesame oil, tomato sauce and spring onion in a small bowl.

2 Pour over the chicken wings, cover and marinate in the refrigerator for at least 2 hours.

3 Place the chicken on a barbecue grill plate or flat plate and cook, in batches, turning once, for 20–25 minutes, or until cooked and golden brown. Baste with the marinade during cooking. Heat any remaining marinade in a saucepan until boiling and serve as a sauce.

NOTE: *The chicken can also be baked in a 180°C (350°F/Gas 4) oven for 30 minutes (turn once).*

Mix together the garlic, hoisin, soy, honey, sesame oil, tomato sauce and spring onion.

Pour the marinade over the chicken wings and marinate in the fridge.

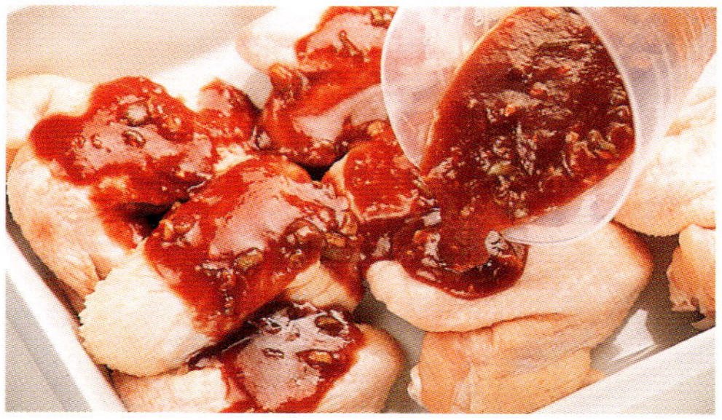

Cook the chicken wings in batches on a barbecue grill plate or flat plate, or bake in the oven.

Chilli con pollo

PREPARATION TIME: 10 MINUTES | TOTAL COOKING TIME: 45 MINUTES | SERVES 4

1 tablespoon olive oil
1 onion, finely chopped
500 g (1 lb 2 oz) minced (ground) chicken
1–2 teaspoons mild chilli powder
440 g (15½ oz) tin chopped tomatoes
2 tablespoons tomato paste (concentrated purée)
1–2 teaspoons soft brown sugar
425 g (15 oz) tin red kidney beans, drained and rinsed

1 Heat the oil in a large saucepan. Add the onion and cook over medium heat for 3 minutes, or until soft. Increase the heat and add the chicken. Cook for 6–8 minutes, or until browned, breaking up any lumps with a wooden spoon.

2 Add the chilli powder and cook for 1 minute. Add the tomato, tomato paste and 125 ml (4 fl oz/½ cup) water and stir well.

3 Bring to the boil, then reduce the heat and simmer for 30 minutes. Stir through the sugar to taste and the kidney beans and heat through. Season and serve with baked corn chips and low-fat natural yoghurt.

NUTRITION PER SERVE
Protein 37 g; Fat 8.5 g; Carbohydrate 20 g; Dietary Fibre 9 g; Cholesterol 60 mg; 1305 kJ (312 Cal)

Cook the chicken until it has browned, breaking up any lumps with a wooden spoon.

Add the tomato, tomato paste and water and stir well to combine.

Simmer for 30 minutes, then stir in the kidney beans and heat through.

Chicken provençale

PREPARATION TIME: 15 MINUTES | TOTAL COOKING TIME: 1 HOUR 20 MINUTES | SERVES 6

1 tablespoon olive oil
1.5 kg (3 lb 5 oz) chicken pieces
1 onion, chopped
1 red capsicum (pepper), chopped
4 tablespoons dry white wine
4 tablespoons chicken stock
425 g (15 oz) tin chopped tomatoes
2 tablespoons tomato paste
(concentrated purée)
90 g (3¼ oz/½ cup) black olives
small handful basil, shredded

1 Heat the oil in a saucepan over high heat, add the chicken, in batches, and cook for 3–4 minutes, or until browned. Return all the chicken to the pan and add the onion and capsicum. Cook for 2–3 minutes, or until the onion is soft.

2 Add the wine, stock, tomato, tomato paste and olives and bring to the boil. Reduce the heat, cover and simmer for 30 minutes. Remove the lid, turn the chicken pieces over and cook for another 30 minutes, or until the chicken is tender and the sauce thickened. Season to taste, sprinkle with the basil and serve with rice.

Once the chicken is browned, return it all to the pan with the onion and capsicum.

Just before serving season then sprinkle with the shredded basil.

NUTRITION PER SERVE
Protein 35 g; Fat 10 g; Carbohydrate 5 g; Dietary Fibre 2 g; Cholesterol 115 mg; 1133 kJ (270 Cal)

Spicy garlic chicken

PREPARATION TIME: 30 MINUTES | TOTAL COOKING TIME: 1 HOUR | SERVES 6

1.4 kg (3 lb 2 oz) chicken pieces
1 small bunch coriander (cilantro)
1 tablespoon olive oil
4 garlic cloves, crushed
2 red onions, thinly sliced
1 large red capsicum (pepper), cut into squares
1 teaspoon ground ginger
1 teaspoon chilli powder
1 teaspoon caraway seeds, crushed
1 teaspoon ground turmeric
2 teaspoons ground coriander
2 teaspoons ground cumin
60 g (2¼ oz/½ cup) raisins
90 g (3¼ oz/½ cup) black olives
1 teaspoon finely grated lemon zest

1 Remove any fat and sinew from the chicken (if you prefer, remove the skin as well). Finely chop the coriander, including the roots.

2 Heat the oil in a large heavy-based saucepan. Add the garlic, onion, capsicum, ginger, chilli powder, caraway seeds, turmeric, ground coriander, cumin and chopped coriander. Cook over medium heat for 10 minutes.

3 Add the chicken pieces and stir until combined. Add 375 ml (13 fl oz/1½ cups) water and bring to the boil. Reduce the heat and simmer for 45 minutes, or until the chicken is tender and cooked through.

4 Add the raisins, black olives and lemon zest and simmer for a further 5 minutes before serving.

VARIATION: *You can use a whole chicken for this recipe and cut it into 12 pieces yourself.*

NUTRITION PER SERVE
Protein 33 g; Fat 13 g; Carbohydrate 13 g; Dietary Fibre 2 g; Cholesterol 105 mg; 1236 kJ (295 Cal)

Wash the coriander and finely chop the whole bunch, including the roots.

Heat the oil in a large saucepan. Add the garlic, onion, capsicum and spices.

Add the chicken pieces to the pan and stir until mixed through.

Lemongrass chicken skewers

PREPARATION TIME: 20 MINUTES + OVERNIGHT MARINATING | TOTAL COOKING TIME: 20 MINUTES | SERVES 4

4 boneless, skinless chicken thighs
1½ tablespoons soft brown sugar
1½ tablespoons lime juice
2 teaspoons green curry paste
18 makrut (kaffir lime) leaves
2 lemongrass stems

MANGO SALSA
1 small mango, finely diced
1 teaspoon grated lime zest
2 teaspoons lime juice
1 teaspoon soft brown sugar
½ teaspoon fish sauce

1 Cut the fat from the chicken and cut the fillets in half lengthways. Combine the brown sugar, lime juice, curry paste and two of the makrut leaves, shredded, in a bowl. Add the chicken and mix well. Cover and refrigerate overnight, or for several hours.

2 Trim the lemongrass to measure about 20 cm (8 inches), leaving the root end intact. Cut each lengthways into four pieces. Cut a slit in each of the remaining makrut leaves and thread one onto each skewer. Cut two slits in the chicken and thread onto the lemongrass, followed by another makrut leaf. Repeat with the remaining makrut leaves, chicken and lemongrass. Pan-fry or barbecue until cooked through.

3 To make the mango salsa, put all the ingredients in a bowl and stir gently to combine. Serve with the chicken skewers.

Discard any fat from the chicken thighs and cut them in half lengthways

Thread a makrut leaf, then the chicken and another makrut leaf onto the skewers.

NUTRITION PER SERVE
Protein 25 g; Fat 2.5 g; Carbohydrate 15 g; Dietary Fibre 1 g; Cholesterol 50 mg; 710 kJ (170 Cal)

Chicken and asparagus stir-fry

PREPARATION TIME: 15 MINUTES | TOTAL COOKING TIME: 10 MINUTES | SERVES 4

1 tablespoon oil
1 garlic clove, crushed
10 cm (4 inch) piece fresh ginger, peeled and thinly sliced
3 boneless, skinless chicken breasts, sliced
4 spring onions (scallions), sliced
200 g (7 oz) asparagus spears, cut into short pieces
2 tablespoons soy sauce
40 g (1½ oz/⅓ cup) slivered almonds, roasted

1 Heat a wok or large frying pan over high heat, add the oil and swirl to coat. Add the garlic, ginger and chicken and stir-fry for 1–2 minutes, or until the chicken changes colour.

2 Add the spring onion and asparagus and stir-fry for a further 2 minutes, or until the spring onion is soft.

3 Stir in the soy sauce and 3 tablespoons water, cover and simmer for 2 minutes, or until the chicken is tender and the vegetables are slightly crisp. Sprinkle with the almonds and serve over steamed rice.

NUTRITION PER SERVE
Protein 22 g; Fat 12 g; Carbohydrate 2 g; Dietary Fibre 2 g; Cholesterol 39 mg; 855 kJ (204 Cal)

Stir-fry the garlic, ginger and chicken until the chicken changes colour.

Add the spring onion and asparagus and stir-fry until the spring onion is soft.

Stir in the soy sauce and water, cover and simmer for a couple of minutes.

Chicken with roasted red capsicum sauce

PREPARATION TIME: 30 MINUTES | TOTAL COOKING TIME: 1 HOUR 15 MINUTES | SERVES 4

2 red capsicums (peppers)
1 tablespoon olive oil
1 red onion, roughly chopped
1–2 garlic cloves, crushed
425 g (15 oz) tin chopped tomatoes
3 large handfuls parsley, chopped
1 very large handful basil leaves, chopped
1 tablespoon tomato paste (concentrated purée)
1 tablespoon caster (superfine) sugar
4 boneless, skinless chicken breasts
spring onion (scallion), chopped, to garnish

NUTRITION PER SERVE
Protein 27 g; Fat 7.5 g; Carbohydrate 9 g; Dietary Fibre 2 g; Cholesterol 55 mg; 886 kJ (210 Cal)

1 Cut the capsicums into quarters, remove the membrane and seeds and grill (broil), skin side up, until blackened. Cool in a plastic bag for 10 minutes, peel away the skin and chop roughly.

2 Heat the oil in a saucepan and cook the onion and garlic for 2 minutes, or until soft but not brown. Add the tomato, parsley, basil, tomato paste, sugar and 375 ml (13 fl oz/ 1½ cups) water.

3 Add the capsicum and cook, stirring often, over very low heat for 45 minutes to 1 hour, or until thick. Leave to cool slightly, then purée in batches in a food processor. Season with salt and pepper.

4 Grill the chicken under a preheated grill (broiler) for 5 minutes on each side, or until cooked through and tender. Serve with the sauce, garnished with spring onion.

Once the capsicum skin has been blackened it should peel away easily.

Cook the onion and garlic until they are softened but not browned.

Add the chopped capsicum to the sauce and cook for up to 1 hour, or until thick.

Chinese braised chicken

PREPARATION TIME: 10 MINUTES | TOTAL COOKING TIME: 1 HOUR | SERVES 6

250 ml (9 fl oz/1 cup) soy sauce
1 cinnamon stick
75 g (2¾ oz/⅓ cup) sugar
4 tablespoons balsamic vinegar
2.5 cm (1 inch) piece fresh ginger, thinly sliced
4 garlic cloves
¼ teaspoon chilli flakes
1.5 kg (3 lb 5 oz) chicken pieces on the bone (skin removed)
1 tablespoon toasted sesame seeds, to garnish

1 Combine 1 litre (35 fl oz/4 cups) water with the soy sauce, cinnamon, sugar, vinegar, ginger, garlic and chilli flakes in a saucepan. Bring to the boil, then reduce the heat and simmer for 5 minutes.

2 Add the chicken and simmer, covered, for 50 minutes, or until cooked through. Serve on a bed of steamed greens and sprinkle with toasted sesame seeds.

NUTRITION PER SERVE
Protein 47.6 g; Fat 15.1 g; Carbohydrate 21.3 g; Dietary Fibre 1 g; Cholesterol 166 mg; 1751 kJ (418 Cal)

Poach the chicken in the Chinese-flavoured liquid until it is cooked through.

Tandoori chicken

PREPARATION TIME: 10 MINUTES + 1 HOUR MARINATING | TOTAL COOKING TIME: 15 MINUTES | SERVES 4

125 g (4½ oz/½ cup) Greek-style low-fat natural yoghurt
2 tablespoons tandoori paste
2 garlic cloves, crushed
2 tablespoons lime juice
1½ teaspoons garam masala
2 tablespoons finely chopped coriander (cilantro) leaves
6 boneless, skinless chicken thighs, fat removed

1 Combine the yoghurt, tandoori paste, garlic, lime juice, garam masala and coriander in a bowl and mix well.

2 Add the chicken, coat well, cover and refrigerate for at least 1 hour.

3 Preheat a barbecue grill plate or flat plate and lightly brush with oil. Cook the chicken, in batches if necessary, for 10–15 minutes on medium heat, turning once and basting with the remaining marinade until golden and cooked through. Serve with cucumber raita and naan bread.

NUTRITION PER SERVE
Protein 36.1 g; Fat 13.4 g; Carbohydrate 4.9 g; Dietary Fibre 0.6 g; Cholesterol 158 mg; 1198 kJ (286 Cal)

Mix together the yoghurt, tandoori paste, garlic, lime juice, garam masala and coriander.

Add the chicken, coating well, and leave in the marinade for at least 1 hour.

Cook the chicken on a hotplate, turning once and basting with the remaining marinade.

Chicken cacciatore

PREPARATION TIME: 20 MINUTES | TOTAL COOKING TIME: 1 HOUR 15 MINUTES | SERVES 6

1 tablespoon olive oil
1 kg (2 lb 4 oz) chicken pieces
2 tablespoons plain (all-purpose) flour
1 large onion, finely chopped
2 garlic cloves, chopped
2 x 425 g (15 oz) tins tomatoes
500 ml (17 fl oz/2 cups) chicken stock
125 ml (4 fl oz/½ cup) dry white wine
2 tablespoons tomato paste (concentrated purée)
1 teaspoon caster (superfine) sugar
3 tablespoons black olives
2 tablespoons chopped basil
2 tablespoons chopped parsley

1 Heat the oil in a saucepan over high heat, add the chicken, in batches, and cook for 3–4 minutes, or until browned. Remove from the pan and sprinkle with flour.

2 Add the onion and garlic to the pan and cook for 10 minutes over low heat, stirring occasionally. Add the tomatoes and their juice, the chicken stock and wine. Bring to the boil and then reduce the heat and simmer for 15 minutes. Add the tomato paste, sugar and chicken and stir well.

3 Cover and simmer for 30 minutes over low heat. Add the olives and herbs, season and simmer for a further 15 minutes, stirring occasionally.

VARIATION: *It is traditional to add a few chopped anchovy fillets just before serving.*

NUTRITION PER SERVE
Protein 30 g; Fat 10 g; Carbohydrate 10 g; Dietary Fibre 3 g; Cholesterol 90 mg; 1100 kJ (265 Cal)

Remove the browned chicken from the pan and sprinkle with flour.

Add the tomato paste, sugar and chicken pieces to the pan.

Stir in the olives, basil and parsley and taste to check the seasoning.

Chicken chasseur

PREPARATION TIME: 20 MINUTES | TOTAL COOKING TIME: 1 HOUR 30 MINUTES | SERVES 4

1 kg (2 lb 4 oz) boneless, skinless chicken thighs
1 tablespoon oil
1 garlic clove, crushed
1 large onion, sliced
100 g (3½ oz) button mushrooms, sliced
1 teaspoon thyme leaves
400 g (14 oz) tin chopped tomatoes
3 tablespoons chicken stock
3 tablespoons dry white wine
1 tablespoon tomato paste (concentrated purée)

1 Preheat the oven to 180°C (350°F/Gas 4). Trim the chicken of any fat and sinew. Heat the oil in a heavy-based frying pan. Add the chicken in batches, and cook for 4 minutes on each side, or until browned. Remove and transfer to a casserole dish.

2 Add the garlic, onion and mushrooms to the pan and cook over medium heat for 5 minutes, or until soft. Add to the chicken with the thyme and tomato.

3 Combine the stock, wine and tomato paste and pour over the chicken. Cover and bake for 1¼ hours, or until the chicken is tender and cooked through.

STORAGE TIME: *Best cooked a day in advance to let the flavours develop.*

Brown the chicken in the hot oil over medium heat and drain on paper towels.

Add the garlic, onion and mushrooms to the pan and cook until soft.

NUTRITION PER SERVE
Protein 60 g; Fat 12 g; Carbohydrate 6 g; Dietary Fibre 2 g; Cholesterol 125 mg; 1710 kJ (410 Cal)

Coq au vin

PREPARATION TIME: 15 MINUTES | TOTAL COOKING TIME: 1 HOUR 40 MINUTES | SERVES 6

1 tablespoon olive oil
125 g (4½ oz) bacon, rind removed, roughly chopped
1.5 kg (3 lb 5 oz) boneless, skinless chicken pieces
350 g (12 oz) baby onions (use bulb or pickling onions)
2 tablespoons plain (all-purpose) flour
750 ml (26 fl oz/3 cups) dry red wine
250 g (9 oz) field mushrooms, sliced
1 tablespoon thyme leaves, to garnish

1 Preheat the oven to 180°C (350°F/Gas 4). Heat the oil in a large ovenproof casserole dish. Add the bacon and cook for 5 minutes, or until golden, then remove. Add the chicken and cook, in batches, for 4–5 minutes, or until browned. Remove. Add the onions and cook for 2–3 minutes, or until browned, then remove from the casserole dish.

2 Add the flour to the casserole dish and stir well, remove from the heat and slowly stir in the red wine. Return to the heat, bring to the boil and return the bacon and chicken to the dish. Cover and cook in the oven for 1 hour. Return the onions to the dish and add the mushrooms. Cook for a further 30 minutes. Season to taste and garnish with the thyme. Serve with crusty bread or pasta.

Cook the onions for a couple of minutes, or until they are browned.

Bring the red wine to the boil, then return the bacon and chicken to the casserole dish.

NUTRITION PER SERVE
Protein 65 g; Fat 11 g; Carbohydrate 11 g; Dietary Fibre 2 g; Cholesterol 150 mg; 2040 kJ (487 Cal)

Chicken meatballs

PREPARATION TIME: 15 MINUTES | TOTAL COOKING TIME: 30 MINUTES | SERVES 6

500 g (1 lb 2 oz) minced (ground) chicken
3 tablespoons fresh breadcrumbs
2 teaspoons finely chopped thyme
1 tablespoon oil
1 onion, finely chopped
2 x 425 g (15 oz) tins chopped tomatoes
2 teaspoons balsamic vinegar
250 ml (9 fl oz/1 cup) chicken stock
grated parmesan cheese, to serve

1 Combine the chicken, breadcrumbs and thyme in a large bowl and season well. Roll tablespoons of the mixture between your hands to make meatballs.

2 Heat the oil in a large non-stick frying pan and cook the meatballs in batches for 5–8 minutes, or until golden brown. Remove from the pan and drain well on paper towels.

3 Add the onion to the pan and cook for 2–3 minutes, or until softened. Add the tomato, vinegar and stock, return the meatballs to the pan, then reduce the heat and simmer for 10 minutes, or until the sauce thickens and the meatballs are cooked through. Serve with pasta and a little parmesan.

NUTRITION PER SERVE
Protein 20 g; Fat 8.5 g; Carbohydrate 7.5 g; Dietary Fibre 2 g; Cholesterol 42 mg; 812 kJ (194 Cal)

Roll tablespoonfuls of the mixture between your hands to make meatballs.

Fry the meatballs in batches until golden brown, then drain well on paper towels.

Return the meatballs to the pan and simmer in the tomato sauce for 10 minutes.

Orange and rosemary glazed chicken

PREPARATION TIME: 10 MINUTES + 4 HOURS MARINATING | TOTAL COOKING TIME: 50 MINUTES | SERVES 6

2 seedless oranges
175 g (6 oz/½ cup) honey
2 tablespoons dijon mustard
1½ tablespoons chopped rosemary
4 garlic cloves, crushed
1.5 kg (3 lb 5 oz) chicken pieces

1 Squeeze the juice from one orange into a bowl, add the honey, dijon mustard, rosemary and garlic and mix together well. Cut the other orange in half and then cut it into slices.

2 Add the chicken and orange slices to the orange juice mixture. Season and mix well and leave to marinate for at least 4 hours. Preheat the oven to 200°C (400°F/Gas 6). Line a large roasting tin with foil. Arrange the chicken and the marinade in the roasting tin.

3 Bake for 40–50 minutes, or until the chicken is golden, turning once and basting with the marinade.

NUTRITION PER SERVE
Protein 40 g; Fat 8.5 g; Carbohydrate 27 g; Dietary Fibre 1 g; Cholesterol 138 mg; 1470 kJ (350 Cal)

Mix together the orange juice, honey, dijon mustard, rosemary and garlic.

Arrange the chicken and marinade in a large roasting tin lined with foil.

Bake the chicken until it is golden, turning once and basting with the marinade.

Chicken with tomato and mango chutney

PREPARATION TIME: 10 MINUTES + 2 HOURS MARINATING | TOTAL COOKING TIME: 45 MINUTES | SERVES 4

8 chicken drumsticks, scored
1 tablespoon mustard powder
2 tablespoons tomato sauce (ketchup)
1 tablespoon sweet mango chutney
1 teaspoon worcestershire sauce
1 tablespoon dijon mustard
30 g (1 oz/¼ cup) raisins
1 tablespoon oil

1 Preheat the oven to 200°C (400°F/Gas 6). Toss the chicken in the mustard powder and season.

2 Combine the tomato sauce, chutney, worcestershire sauce, mustard, raisins and oil. Spoon over the chicken and toss well to coat evenly. Marinate for 2 hours, or overnight, turning once.

3 Put the chicken in a shallow roasting tin and bake for 45 minutes, or until the meat comes away from the bone.

SERVING SUGGESTION: *Serve with toasted Turkish bread and a mixture of yoghurt, cucumber and mint.*

NUTRITION PER SERVE
Protein 25 g; Fat 15 g; Carbohydrate 3.5 g; Dietary Fibre 0.5 g; Cholesterol 103 mg; 1005 kJ (240 Cal)

The cleanest way to toss the chicken in mustard powder is to put them in a plastic bag.

Marinate the chicken for at least 2 hours, turning it over once.

Bake the chicken for 45 minutes, or until the meat is coming away from the bone.

Chargrilled chicken

PREPARATION TIME: 20 MINUTES + 2 HOURS REFRIGERATION | TOTAL COOKING TIME: 50 MINUTES | SERVES 4

4 boneless, skinless chicken breasts
2 tablespoons honey
1 tablespoon wholegrain mustard
1 tablespoon soy sauce
2 red onions, cut into wedges
8 roma (plum) tomatoes, halved lengthways
2 tablespoons soft brown sugar
2 tablespoons balsamic vinegar
cooking oil spray

1 Preheat the oven to 180°C (350°F/ Gas 4). Trim the chicken of any fat and place in a shallow dish. Combine the honey, mustard and soy sauce and pour over the chicken, tossing to coat. Cover and refrigerate for 2 hours, turning once.

2 Place the onion wedges and tomato halves on a baking tray covered with baking paper. Sprinkle with the sugar and drizzle with the balsamic vinegar. Bake for 40 minutes.

3 Heat a chargrill pan or hotplate and lightly spray with oil. Remove the chicken from the marinade and cook for 4–5 minutes on each side, or until cooked through. Slice and serve with the tomato halves and onion wedges.

NUTRITION PER SERVE
Protein 25 g; Fat 2.5 g; Carbohydrate 30 g; Dietary Fibre 3 g; Cholesterol 50 mg; 990 kJ (235 Cal)

Pour the marinade over the chicken and toss to coat thoroughly.

Drizzle the balsamic vinegar over the onion and tomato in the baking tray.

Cook the marinated chicken in a hot, lightly oiled chargrill pan or hotplate.

Sweet chilli chicken

PREPARATION TIME: 15 MINUTES + 2 HOURS REFRIGERATION | TOTAL COOKING TIME: 20 MINUTES | SERVES 6

1 kg (2 lb 4 oz) boneless, skinless chicken thighs
2 tablespoons lime juice
125 ml (4 fl oz/½ cup) sweet chilli sauce
3 tablespoons kecap manis (see NOTE, page 13)

1 Trim any excess fat from the chicken thighs and cut them in half. Put the chicken in a shallow non-metallic dish.

2 Place the lime juice, sweet chilli sauce and kecap manis in a bowl and whisk to combine.

3 Pour the marinade over the chicken, cover and refrigerate for 2 hours.

4 Chargrill or bake the chicken in a 200°C (400°F/Gas 6) oven for 20 minutes, or until the chicken is tender and cooked through and the marinade has caramelised.

NUTRITION PER SERVE
Protein 35 g; Fat 4.5 g; Carbohydrate 4 g; Dietary Fibre 1 g; Cholesterol 85 mg; 880 kJ (210 Cal)

Trim the excess fat from the thigh fillets and cut them in half.

To make the marinade, whisk together the lime juice, sweet chilli sauce and kecap manis.

Pour the marinade over the chicken, then cover and refrigerate.

Chicken mole

PREPARATION TIME: 25 MINUTES | TOTAL COOKING TIME: 1 HOUR | SERVES 4

8 chicken drumsticks
plain (all-purpose) flour, for dusting
cooking oil spray
1 large onion, finely chopped
2 garlic cloves, finely chopped
1 teaspoon ground cumin
1 teaspoon Mexican chilli powder
2 teaspoons cocoa powder
250 ml (9 fl oz/1 cup) chicken stock
2 x 440 g (15½ oz) tins tomatoes, chopped
almonds, to garnish

1 Remove and discard the chicken skin. Wipe the chicken with paper towels and lightly dust with flour. Spray a large, deep, non-stick frying pan with oil. Cook the chicken for 8 minutes over high heat, turning until golden brown. Remove and set aside.

2 Add the onion, garlic, cumin, chilli powder, cocoa, 1 teaspoon salt, ½ teaspoon black pepper and 3 tablespoons water to the pan and cook for 5 minutes, or until softened.

3 Stir in the stock and tomato. Bring to the boil, add the chicken drumsticks, cover and simmer for 45 minutes, or until tender. Uncover and simmer for 5 minutes, until the mixture is thick. Garnish with the almonds.

NOTE: *This Mexican dish is usually flavoured with a special type of dark chocolate rather than cocoa powder.*

Pull the skin off the chicken drumsticks, then wipe the chicken with paper towels.

Turn the chicken until brown on all sides, then remove from the pan.

NUTRITION PER SERVE
Protein 25 g; Fat 7 g; Carbohydrate 10 g; Dietary Fibre 4 g; Cholesterol 100 mg; 910 kJ (220 Cal)

Seafood

Sardines with chargrilled capsicum and eggplant

PREPARATION TIME: 25 MINUTES | TOTAL COOKING TIME: 35 MINUTES | SERVES 4

2 large red capsicums (peppers), quartered and seeded
4 long thin eggplants (aubergines), cut into quarters lengthways
cooking oil spray

DRESSING
1 tablespoon olive oil
1 tablespoon balsamic vinegar
½ teaspoon soft brown sugar
1 garlic clove, crushed
1 tablespoon snipped fresh chives

16 fresh sardines, butterflied (about 300 g/10½ oz)
1 slice white bread, crusts removed
1 medium handful parsley
1 garlic clove, crushed
1 teaspoon grated lemon zest

1 Preheat the oven to 180°C (350°F/Gas 4). Lightly grease a large baking dish with oil. Preheat the grill (broiler) and line with foil.

2 Grill (broil) the capsicum until the skin is blistered and blackened. Cool in a plastic bag for 10 minutes, peel away the skin and slice thickly lengthways. Lightly spray the eggplant with oil and grill (broil) each side for 3–5 minutes, until softened.

3 Combine the dressing ingredients in a screw-top jar and shake well. Put the capsicum and eggplant in a bowl, pour the dressing over, toss well and set aside.

4 Place the sardines on a baking tray in a single layer, well spaced. Finely chop the bread, parsley, garlic and lemon zest together in a food processor. Sprinkle over each sardine. Bake for 10–15 minutes, until cooked through. Serve with the capsicum and eggplant.

NUTRITION PER SERVE
Protein 20 g; Fat 15 g; Carbohydrate 15 g; Dietary Fibre 3 g; Cholesterol 85 mg; 1185 kJ (285 Cal)

When the capsicum has cooled enough to handle, peel away the skin.

Pour the dressing over the capsicum and eggplant, then toss.

Sprinkle the chopped bread, parsley, garlic and lemon zest over the sardines.

Pasta puttanesca

PREPARATION TIME: 20 MINUTES | TOTAL COOKING TIME: 20 MINUTES | SERVES 4

500 g (1 lb 2 oz) pasta
1 tablespoon olive oil
3 garlic cloves
2 tablespoons chopped parsley
¼–½ teaspoon chilli flakes or powder
2 x 425 g (15 oz) tins chopped tomatoes
1 tablespoon capers, drained and well rinsed
3 anchovy fillets, thinly sliced
45 g (1½ oz/¼ cup) black olives

1 Cook the pasta in a large pan of rapidly boiling salted water until *al dente*. Drain and return to the pan.

2 While the pasta is cooking, heat the oil in a large heavy-based saucepan. Chop the garlic, then finely crush with the flat side of a knife. Add the garlic, parsley and chilli flakes and stir constantly for about 1 minute, over medium heat.

3 Add the tomato to the pan and bring to the boil. Reduce the heat and simmer, covered, for 5 minutes.

4 Add the capers, anchovies and olives and stir for another 5 minutes. Season with black pepper. Add the sauce to the pasta and toss gently. Serve with a little parmesan, if desired.

Squash each clove of garlic with the flat side of a knife, pressing with the palm of your hand.

Roughly chop the garlic, with a little salt, then scrape the knife at an angle to finely crush.

NUTRITION PER SERVE:
Protein 20 g; Fat 15 g; Carbohydrate 95 g; Dietary Fibre 9 g; Cholesterol 8 mg; 2510 kJ (595 Cal)

Cod with papaya and black bean salsa

PREPARATION TIME: 25 MINUTES | TOTAL COOKING TIME: 5 MINUTES | SERVES 4

1 small red onion, finely chopped
1 papaya (about 500 g/1 lb 2 oz), peeled, seeded and cubed
1 bird's-eye chilli (pepper), seeded and finely chopped
1 tablespoon salted black beans, drained and rinsed
cooking oil spray
4 blue-eyed cod cutlets
2 teaspoons peanut oil
1 teaspoon sesame oil
2 teaspoons fish sauce
1 tablespoon lime juice
1 tablespoon chopped fresh coriander (cilantro) leaves
2 teaspoons shredded fresh mint

1 Toss together the onion, papaya, chilli and black beans.

2 Heat a chargrill pan or plate and lightly spray with oil. Add the cod and cook for 2 minutes each side, or until cooked to your liking.

3 Whisk together the peanut oil, sesame oil, fish sauce and lime juice. Pour over the papaya and black bean salsa and toss. Add the coriander and mint and serve immediately, at room temperature, with the fish.

NOTE: *Black beans have a distinctive taste, so if you are not familiar with them, taste them before adding to the salsa. If you prefer not to add them, the salsa is equally delicious without.*

VARIATION: *Pawpaw can be used instead of papaya. It is a larger fruit from the same family, with yellower flesh and a less sweet flavour.*

NUTRITION PER SERVE
Protein 18 g; Fat 6 g; Carbohydrate 5 g; Dietary Fibre 1 g; Cholesterol 40 mg; 540 kJ (130 Cal)

Cut the papaya in half and scoop out the seeds with a spoon.

The best way to toss the salsa, without breaking up the fruit, is with your hands.

Seafood and herb risotto

PREPARATION TIME: 40 MINUTES | TOTAL COOKING TIME: 50 MINUTES | SERVES 4

150 g (5½ oz) white boneless fish fillet, such as sea perch
8 black mussels, about 200 g (7 oz)
8 raw prawns (shrimp), about 250 g (9 oz)
1.75 litres (61 fl oz/7 cups) chicken stock
cooking oil spray
2 onions, finely chopped
2 garlic cloves, finely chopped
1 celery stalk, finely chopped
440 g (15½ oz/2 cups) arborio rice
2 tablespoons chopped parsley
1 tablespoon chopped oregano
1 tablespoon chopped thyme leaves
2 tablespoons grated parmesan cheese

NUTRITION PER SERVE
Protein 40 g; Fat 5 g; Carbohydrate 90 g; Dietary Fibre 4 g; Cholesterol 175 mg; 2395 kJ (570 Cal)

1 Cut the fish into small cubes. Scrub the mussels well and remove the beards. Discard any broken mussels, or open ones that don't close when tapped on the work surface. Rinse well. Peel and devein the prawns, leaving the tails intact. Put the seafood in a bowl and refrigerate until required.

2 Put the stock in a saucepan and bring to the boil. Reduce the heat until just simmering.

3 Spray a large saucepan with oil and heat over medium heat. Add the onion, garlic and celery and cook for 2–3 minutes. Add 2 tablespoons water, cover and cook for 5 minutes. Add the arborio rice and 2 tablespoons water and stir over medium heat for 3–4 minutes. Gradually add 125 ml (4 fl oz/½ cup) of the stock to the rice, stirring constantly over low heat, until all the stock has been absorbed. Repeat, adding 125 ml of stock each time until all but a small amount of stock is left and the rice is just tender.

4 Meanwhile, bring a small amount of water to the boil in a saucepan. Add the mussels, cover and cook for about 3 minutes, shaking the pan occasionally, until the mussels have opened. Drain, and discard any that did not open.

5 Add the fish and prawns and the remaining stock to the rice. Stir well and continue to cook for about 5–10 minutes, or until the seafood is just cooked. Remove from the heat, add the cooked mussels, cover and set aside for 5 minutes. Stir the herbs and parmesan through the risotto, then season well. Serve immediately.

Scrub the mussels thoroughly and pull off the beards. Discard any open mussels.

Add the arborio rice to the pan and stir over the heat until the rice is well coated.

Risotto is ready when the rice has absorbed all the hot stock.

Thai-style whole snapper

PREPARATION TIME: 10 MINUTES | TOTAL COOKING TIME: 30 MINUTES | SERVES 6

2 garlic cloves, crushed
1 tablespoon fish sauce
2 tablespoons lemon juice
1 tablespoon grated fresh ginger
2 tablespoons sweet chilli sauce
2 tablespoons chopped coriander (cilantro)
1 tablespoon rice wine vinegar
2 tablespoons dry white wine
600 g (1 lb 5 oz) whole snapper, cleaned and scaled (ask your fishmonger to do this)
2 spring onions (scallions), cut into thin strips

1 Preheat the oven to 190°C (375°F/Gas 5). Place the garlic, fish sauce, lemon juice, ginger, chilli sauce, coriander, vinegar and wine in a bowl and mix together well.

2 Place the snapper on a large piece of foil on a baking tray. Pour the marinade over the fish and sprinkle with the spring onion.

3 Wrap the foil around the fish like a parcel and place in the oven. Bake for 20–30 minutes or until the flesh flakes easily when tested with a fork. Serve immediately with steamed rice.

NUTRITION PER SERVE
Protein 20 g; Fat 2 g; Carbohydrate 5 g; Dietary Fibre 0 g; Cholesterol 60 mg; 495 kJ (120 Cal)

Put the ingredients for the marinade in a bowl and mix together well.

Pour the marinade over the snapper after you have placed it on the aluminium foil.

Cook the fish until the flesh flakes easily when tested with a fork.

Mussels in chunky tomato sauce

PREPARATION TIME: 15 MINUTES | TOTAL COOKING TIME: 30 MINUTES | SERVES 6

1.5 kg (3 lb 5 oz) black mussels
1 tablespoon olive oil
1 large onion, diced
4 garlic cloves, finely chopped
2 x 400 g (14 oz) tins chopped tomatoes
60 g (2¼ oz/¼ cup) tomato paste (concentrated purée)
30 g (1 oz/¼ cup) pitted black olives
1 tablespoon capers, drained and well rinsed
125 ml (4 fl oz/½ cup) fish stock
3 tablespoons chopped parsley

1 Scrub the mussels with a stiff brush and pull out the hairy beards. Discard any broken mussels, or open ones that don't close when tapped on the work surface. Rinse well.

2 In a large saucepan, heat the olive oil and cook the onion and garlic over medium heat for 1–2 minutes, until softened. Add the tomato, tomato paste, olives, capers and fish stock. Bring to the boil, then reduce the heat and simmer, stirring occasionally, for 20 minutes, or until the sauce is thick.

3 Stir in the mussels and cover the saucepan. Shake or toss the mussels occasionally and cook for 4–5 minutes, or until the mussels begin to open. Remove the pan from the heat and discard any mussels that haven't opened in the cooking time. Just before serving, toss the parsley through.

Simmer the chunky tomato sauce, stirring occasionally, until thick.

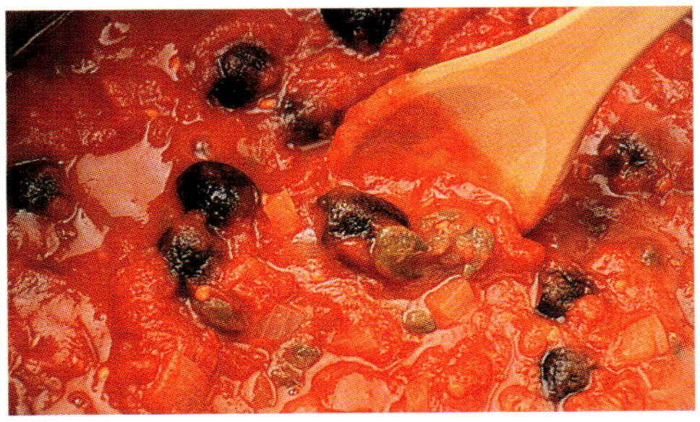

Cook the mussels until they open. Discard any that don't open in the cooking time.

NUTRITION PER SERVE
Protein 17 g; Fat 12 g; Carbohydrate 11 g; Dietary Fibre 3 g; Cholesterol 35 mg; 973 kJ (233 Cal)

Crumbed fish with wasabi cream

PREPARATION TIME: 25 MINUTES + 15 MINUTES REFRIGERATION | TOTAL COOKING TIME: 20 MINUTES | SERVES 4

60 g (2¼ oz/¾ cup) fresh breadcrumbs
25 g (1 oz/¾ cup) cornflakes
1 sheet nori (dried seaweed), torn roughly (see NOTE)
¼ teaspoon paprika
4 x 150 g (5½ oz) pieces firm white fish fillets
plain (all-purpose) flour, for dusting
1 egg white
1 tablespoon skim milk
1 spring onion (scallion), thinly sliced

WASABI CREAM
125 g (4½ oz/½ cup) low-fat natural yoghurt
1 teaspoon wasabi (see NOTE)
1 tablespoon low-fat mayonnaise
1 teaspoon lime juice

NUTRITION PER SERVE
Protein 35 g; Fat 6 g; Carbohydrate 25 g; Dietary Fibre 1 g; Cholesterol 105 mg; 1270 kJ (305 Cal)

1 Preheat the oven to 180°C (350°F/Gas 4). Combine the breadcrumbs, cornflakes, nori and paprika in a food processor and process until the nori is finely chopped.

2 Dust the fish lightly with the flour, dip into the combined egg white and milk, then into the breadcrumb mixture. Press the crumb mixture onto the fish firmly, then refrigerate for 15 minutes.

3 Line a baking tray with baking paper and put the fish on the paper. Bake for 15–20 minutes, or until the fish flakes easily with a fork.

4 To make the wasabi cream, mix the ingredients thoroughly in a bowl. Serve with the fish and sprinkle with a little spring onion.

NOTE: *Wasabi paste (a pungent paste, also known as Japanese horseradish) and nori (sheets of paper-thin dried seaweed) are both available from Asian food stores.*

Process the breadcrumbs, cornflakes, nori and paprika together.

Dust the fish with flour, dip in the egg and milk, then press in the breadcrumbs.

Thoroughly mix the wasabi cream ingredients in a bowl and then serve with the fish.

Smoked salmon pizzas

PREPARATION TIME: 20 MINUTES | TOTAL COOKING TIME: 15 MINUTES | SERVES 6

250 g (9 oz/1 cup) low-fat ricotta cheese
6 small oval pitta breads
125 g (4½ oz) sliced smoked salmon
1 small red onion, sliced
1 tablespoon baby capers, drained and well rinsed
small dill sprigs, to garnish
1 lemon, cut into thin wedges, for serving

1 Preheat the oven to 180°C (350°F/Gas 4). Put the ricotta in a bowl, season well with salt and pepper and stir until smooth. Spread the ricotta over the breads, leaving a clear border around the edge.

2 Top each pizza with some smoked salmon slices, then some onion pieces. Scatter baby capers over the top and bake on a baking tray for 15 minutes, or until the bases are slightly crispy around the edges. Garnish with a few dill sprigs and serve with lemon wedges.

NUTRITION PER SERVE
Protein 20 g; Fat 8 g; Carbohydrate 60 g; Dietary Fibre 4 g; Cholesterol 30 mg; 1650 kJ (395 Cal)

Peel the small red onion and then cut it into thin slices.

Spread the seasoned ricotta over the pitta breads, leaving a border around the edge.

Put some smoked salmon slices over the ricotta, followed by onion and capers.

Clams in roasted chilli paste

PREPARATION TIME: 15 MINUTES | TOTAL COOKING TIME: 15 MINUTES | SERVES 4

ROASTED CHILLI PASTE
2 tablespoons oil
2 spring onions (scallions), sliced
2 garlic cloves, sliced
90 g (3¼ oz/¼ cup) small dried shrimp
6 small red chillies, seeded
2 teaspoons palm sugar (jaggery)
2 teaspoons fish sauce
2 teaspoons tamarind concentrate

3 garlic cloves, finely sliced
3 small red chillies, seeded and sliced lengthways
1 tablespoon light soy sauce
250 ml (9 fl oz/1 cup) chicken stock
1 kg (2 lb 4 oz) clams (vongole), scrubbed
1 large handful Thai basil leaves

1 To make the roasted chilli paste, heat the oil in a wok and fry the spring onion, garlic, dried shrimp and chillies until golden brown. Remove with a slotted spoon and keep the oil.

2 Place the onion, garlic, shrimp, chillies and sugar in a mortar and pestle or small food processor and grind until the mixture is well blended. Add the fish sauce, tamarind concentrate and a pinch of salt. Blend or grind to a fine paste. Transfer to a bowl.

3 Heat the reserved oil in the wok. Add the garlic, chilli, roasted chilli paste and soy sauce. Mix well, then add the chicken stock and bring just to the boil. Add the clams and cook over medium–high heat for 2–3 minutes. Discard any unopened clams. Stir in the basil and serve immediately with steamed jasmine rice.

Use a slotted spoon to remove the onion, garlic, shrimps and chillies from the wok.

Remove any clams that have not opened during the cooking time

NUTRITION PER SERVE
Protein 30 g; Fat 15 g; Carbohydrate 90 g; Dietary Fibre 5 g; Cholesterol 280 mg; 2490 kJ (700 Cal)

Calamari with spicy sauce

PREPARATION TIME: 50 MINUTES + 3 HOURS MARINATING | TOTAL COOKING TIME: 7 MINUTES | SERVES 4

500 g (1 lb 2 oz) squid tubes, cleaned
2 lemongrass stems, white part only, finely chopped
3 teaspoons grated fresh ginger
3 garlic cloves, finely chopped
½ teaspoon chopped red chilli
1 tablespoon vegetable oil
2 very ripe tomatoes
150 g (5½ oz) mixed lettuce
1 handful coriander (cilantro) leaves
2 tablespoons lime juice
1 teaspoon finely grated lime zest
1 red capsicum (pepper), cut into strips

LIME, CHILLI AND GARLIC SAUCE

3 tablespoons lime juice
1 tablespoon lemon juice
2 tablespoons fish sauce
1 tablespoon caster (superfine) sugar
2 teaspoons chopped red chilli
2 garlic cloves, finely chopped
1 tablespoon finely chopped coriander (cilantro)

1 Cut the squid tubes open, wash and pat dry. Cut shallow slashes about 5 mm (¼ inch) apart on the soft inside, in a diamond pattern, then cut into 3 cm (1¼ inch) strips. Mix in a bowl with the lemongrass, ginger, garlic, chilli and oil. Cover with plastic wrap and refrigerate for 3 hours.

2 Cut the tomatoes in half, scoop out the membrane and seeds and finely chop them, retaining all the juices. Cut the flesh into small cubes and set aside. Arrange the lettuce and coriander leaves in serving bowls.

3 Just before serving, lightly grease and heat a solid barbecue grill plate or flat plate or large, heavy non-stick frying pan until very hot. Quickly cook the squid in batches, tossing for 2–3 minutes, until just tender and curled, sprinkling the lime juice and zest over the top. Remove the squid, toss with the chopped tomato seeds and arrange on the salad. Scatter the tomato and capsicum over the top. Season well.

4 Stir the sauce ingredients together until the sugar dissolves. Drizzle over the squid.

NUTRITION PER SERVE
Protein 25 g; Fat 6.5 g; Carbohydrate 5 g; Dietary Fibre 3 g; Cholesterol 250 mg; 755 kJ (180 Cal)

Score a shallow diamond pattern on the soft insides of the squid tubes.

Scoop out the tomato membrane and seeds and finely chop the flesh.

Don't overcook the squid or it will be tough, and don't crowd the pan.

Prawn curry

PREPARATION TIME: 25 MINUTES | TOTAL COOKING TIME: 15 MINUTES | SERVES 6

1 tablespoon butter
1 onion, finely chopped
1 garlic clove, crushed
1½ tablespoons curry powder
2 tablespoons plain (all-purpose) flour
500 ml (17 fl oz/2 cups) skim milk
1 kg (2 lb 4 oz) raw prawns (shrimp), peeled and deveined
1½ tablespoons lemon juice
2 teaspoons sherry
1 tablespoon finely chopped parsley

1 Heat the butter in a large saucepan. Add the onion and garlic, and cook for 5 minutes, or until softened. Add the curry powder and cook for 1 minute, then stir in the flour and cook for a further 1 minute.

2 Remove from the heat and stir in the milk until smooth. Return to the heat and stir constantly until the sauce has thickened. Simmer for 2 minutes and then stir in the prawns. Continue to simmer for 5 minutes, or until the prawns are just cooked.

3 Stir in the lemon juice, sherry and parsley and serve immediately with rice.

NUTRITION PER SERVE
Protein 38 g; Fat 12 g; Carbohydrate 9 g; Dietary Fibre 1.5 g; Cholesterol 280 mg; 1247 kJ (298 Cal)

Add the garlic and onion to the butter and cook until softened.

Return the saucepan to the heat and stir the curry constantly until thickened.

Add the prawns and continue to simmer until they are just cooked.

Swordfish with pineapple salsa

PREPARATION TIME: 20 MINUTES + 2 HOURS STANDING | TOTAL COOKING TIME: 5 MINUTES | SERVES 4

375 g (13 oz/2 cups) pineapple, diced
1 small red onion, chopped
1 red capsicum (pepper), chopped
1 jalapeño chilli, seeded
1 tablespoon grated fresh ginger
finely grated zest of 1 lime
1 tablespoon lime juice
1 large handful coriander (cilantro) leaves, chopped
4 swordfish steaks

1 Put the diced pineapple, roughly chopped onion, capsicum, chilli and ginger in a food processor and mix, using the pulse button, until coarsely chopped. Stir in the lime zest and juice and the coriander leaves. Season with salt and pour into a small bowl.

2 Cover and leave the salsa for 2 hours. Meanwhile, soak four wooden skewers in cold water for 30 minutes to prevent scorching. Drain off any excess liquid from the salsa.

3 Cut the swordfish into cubes and thread onto the skewers. Grill under a hot grill (broiler) for 3 minutes on each side, or until cooked through. Serve the skewers with the salsa.

NUTRITION PER SERVE
Protein 21 g; Fat 1 g; Carbohydrate 7 g; Dietary Fibre 2 g; Cholesterol 55 mg; 390 kJ (120 Cal)

Cut away the skin from the pineapple with a sharp knife.

Use the knife to cut out the tough eyes from the flesh of the pineapple.

Process the salsa until coarsely chopped and then stir in the remaining ingredients.

Paella

PREPARATION TIME: 25 MINUTES | TOTAL COOKING TIME: 45 MINUTES | SERVES 6

500 g (1 lb 2 oz) raw prawns (shrimp)
300 g (10½ oz) skinless firm white fish fillets
250 g (9 oz) black mussels
200 g (7 oz) squid rings
2 tablespoons olive oil
1 large onion, diced
3 garlic cloves, finely chopped
1 small red capsicum (pepper), thinly sliced
1 small red chilli, seeded and chopped
2 teaspoons paprika
1 teaspoon ground turmeric
2 tomatoes, peeled and diced
1 tablespoon tomato paste (concentrated purée)
400 g (14 oz/2 cups) long-grain rice
125 ml (4 fl oz/½ cup) dry white wine
1.25 litres (44 fl oz/5 cups) fish stock
3 tablespoons chopped parsley, for serving
lemon wedges, for serving

NUTRITION PER SERVE
Protein 44.5 g; Fat 14.5 g; Carbohydrate 60 g; Dietary Fibre 3.5 g; Cholesterol 217 mg; 2360 kJ (560 Cal)

1 Peel the prawns, leaving the tails intact. Gently pull out the dark vein from each prawn back. Cut the fish into cubes. Scrub the mussels and pull out the hairy beards. Discard any broken mussels, or open ones that don't close when tapped on the work surface. Refrigerate the seafood, covered, until ready to use.

2 Heat the oil in a paella pan or a large deep frying pan with a lid. Add the onion, garlic, capsicum and chilli and cook over medium heat for about 2 minutes. Add the paprika, turmeric and 1 teaspoon salt and stir-fry for 1–2 minutes, or until aromatic. Add the tomato and cook for 5 minutes, or until softened. Add the tomato paste. Stir in the rice until it is well coated. Pour in the wine and simmer until almost absorbed. Add the fish stock and bring to the boil. Reduce the heat and simmer for 20 minutes, or until almost all the liquid is absorbed. There is no need to stir the rice. You may occasionally wish to fluff it up with a fork.

3 Add the mussels to the pan, poking the shells into the rice, cover and cook for 2–3 minutes over low heat. Add the prawns and cook for 2–3 minutes. Add the fish, cover and cook for 3 minutes. Finally, add the squid rings and cook for 1–2 minutes. By this time, the mussels should have opened—discard any unopened ones. The prawns should be pink and the fish should flake easily when tested with a fork. The squid should be moist and tender. Cook for another 2–3 minutes if the seafood is not quite cooked. Serve with parsley and lemon wedges and a green salad.

Peel and pull out the dark vein frcm along the back of each prawn.

Add the rice to the pan and stir with a wooden spoon until well coated.

Cook the squid rings for 1–2 minutes. Don't overcook or they will be tough.

Prawns with jasmine rice

PREPARATION TIME: 15 MINUTES | TOTAL COOKING TIME: 30 MINUTES | SERVES 4

1 tablespoon peanut oil
8 spring onions (scallions), sliced
1 tablespoon finely chopped fresh ginger
1 tablespoon finely sliced lemongrass, white part only
2 teaspoons crushed coriander seeds (see NOTE)
400 g (14 oz/2 cups) jasmine rice
1 litre (35 fl oz/4 cups) vegetable stock
1 tablespoon shredded lime zest
1 kg (2 lb 4 oz) raw prawns (shrimp), peeled, deveined and chopped
2 tablespoons lime juice
2 very large handfuls coriander (cilantro) leaves
fish sauce, for serving

1 Heat the oil in a saucepan, add the spring onion and cook over low heat for 4 minutes, or until soft. Add the ginger, lemongrass, coriander seeds and rice, and stir for 1 minute.

2 Add the stock and lime zest and bring to the boil while stirring. Reduce the heat to very low and cook, covered, for 15–20 minutes, or until the rice is tender.

3 Remove the pan from the heat and stir in the prawns. Cover and leave for 4–5 minutes, or until the prawns are cooked. Add the lime juice and coriander leaves and fluff the rice with a fork. Sprinkle with a few drops of fish sauce to serve.

NOTE: *To crush coriander seeds, place in a small plastic bag and, using a rolling pin, crush until fine.*

Peel and devein the prawns and chop them into small pieces.

Add the ginger, lemongrass, coriander seeds and rice to the saucepan.

NUTRITION PER SERVE
Protein 59 g; Fat 12 g; Carbohydrate 80 g; Dietary Fibre 3 g; Cholesterol 373 mg; 2850 kJ (681 Cal)

Spaghetti with chilli calamari

PREPARATION TIME: 15 MINUTES | TOTAL COOKING TIME: 30 MINUTES | SERVES 4

500 g (1 lb 4 oz) squid, cleaned
500 g (1 lb 4 oz) spaghetti
1 tablespoon olive oil
1 leek, white part only, chopped
2 garlic cloves, crushed
1–2 teaspoons chopped chilli
½ teaspoon cayenne pepper
425 g (15 oz) tin chopped tomatoes
125 ml (4 fl oz/½ cup) fish stock
1 tablespoon chopped basil
2 teaspoons chopped sage
1 teaspoon chopped marjoram

1 Pull the tentacles from the body of the squid. Using your fingers, pull the quill from the pouch of the squid. Pull the skin away from the flesh and discard. Use a sharp knife to slit the tubes up one side. Lay out flat and score one side in a diamond pattern. Cut each tube into four.

2 Cook the spaghetti in a large pan of rapidly boiling salted water until *al dente*. Drain and keep warm.

3 Heat the oil in a large frying pan. Add the leek and cook for 2 minutes. Add the garlic and stir over low heat for 1 minute. Stir in the chilli and cayenne. Add the tomato, stock and herbs and bring to the boil. Reduce the heat and simmer for 5 minutes.

4 Add the squid to the pan. Simmer for another 5–10 minutes, or until tender. Serve the chilli squid over the spaghetti.

NUTRITION PER SERVE
Protein 35 g; Fat 15 g; Carbohydrate 90 g; Dietary Fibre 10 g; Cholesterol 250 mg; 2670 kJ (640 Cal)

Pull the clear quill from the pouch of the squid and then pull the skin away from the flesh.

Add the squid to the pan and simmer for 5–10 minutes, until tender.

Spiced fish wrapped in banana leaves

PREPARATION TIME: 20 MINUTES | TOTAL COOKING TIME: 35 MINUTES | SERVES 6

SPICE PASTE
1 red onion, finely chopped
3 small red chillies, seeded and chopped
1 teaspoon shrimp paste
1 cm (½ inch) piece fresh galangal, finely chopped
1 lemongrass stem, white part only, finely sliced
5 blanched almonds, chopped
4 makrut (kaffir lime) leaves, finely shredded

2 teaspoons sesame oil
1 tablespoon vegetable oil
1 teaspoon soy sauce
1 banana leaf, about 50 cm x 30 cm (20 x 12 inches)
1 whole trout or silver bream, about 750 g (1 lb 10 oz), cleaned and scaled

1 To make the spice paste, grind all the ingredients except the makrut leaves in a food processor with 2 tablespoons water until smooth. Transfer to a bowl and mix in the makrut leaves. Set aside.

2 Preheat the oven to 180°C (350°F/Gas 4). Heat the sesame oil and vegetable oil in a small frying pan and gently fry the spice paste for 5 minutes. Mix in the soy sauce. Remove from the heat and cool.

3 Cut a large rectangle from the banana leaf and brush with oil. Wash the fish well under running water and pat dry. Score the fish several times on both sides and rub in the spice paste, pushing it well into the slits.

4 Place the fish on the banana leaf and fold over to make a parcel. Wrap again in foil to secure. Bake for 25–30 minutes, or until the flesh flakes easily when tested with a fork. Unwrap the fish to serve.

NUTRITION PER SERVE
Protein 30 g; Fat 15 g; Carbohydrate 3 g; Dietary Fibre 1 g; Cholesterol 75 mg; 1050 kJ (250 Cal)

Mix the spice paste until smooth and then add the shredded makrut leaves.

Score the fish several times on both sides with a sharp knife.

Wrap the fish in the banana leaf, folding in the ends securely.

Fusilli with tuna, capers and parsley

PREPARATION TIME: 15 MINUTES | TOTAL COOKING TIME: 10 MINUTES | SERVES 4

425 g (15 oz) can tuna in spring water, drained
2 tablespoons olive oil
2 garlic cloves, finely chopped
2 small red chillies, finely chopped
3 tablespoons capers, drained and well rinsed (see HINT)
2 very large handfuls parsley, finely chopped
3 tablespoons lemon juice
375 g (13 oz) fusilli

1 Place the tuna in a bowl and flake lightly with a fork. Combine the oil, garlic, chilli, capers, parsley and lemon juice. Pour over the tuna and mix lightly. Season well.

2 Meanwhile, cook the pasta in a large saucepan of rapidly boiling salted water until *al dente*. Reserve 125 ml (4 fl oz/½ cup) of the cooking water, then drain the pasta. Toss the tuna mixture through the pasta, adding enough of the reserved water to give a moist consistency. Serve immediately.

HINT: *Generally, the smaller the caper the tastier, so use baby ones if you can find them.*

NUTRITION PER SERVE
Protein 35 g; Fat 13 g; Carbohydrate 65 g; Dietary Fibre 5 g; Cholesterol 55 mg; 2270 kJ (545 Cal)

Finely chop the chillies. Remove the seeds if you prefer a milder taste.

Break the tuna into flakes with a fork and then mix with the dressing.

Cook the pasta in a large saucepan of rapidly boiling salted water.

Tuna with coriander noodles

PREPARATION TIME: 15 MINUTES | TOTAL COOKING TIME: 10 MINUTES | SERVES 4

3 tablespoons lime juice
2 tablespoons fish sauce
2 tablespoons sweet chilli sauce
2 teaspoons grated palm sugar (jaggery)
1 teaspoon sesame oil
1 garlic clove, finely chopped
1 tablespoon virgin olive oil
4 tuna steaks
200 g (7 oz) dried thin wheat noodles
6 spring onions (scallions), thinly sliced
2 large handfuls coriander (cilantro) leaves, chopped, plus extra, to garnish

1 To make the dressing, place the lime juice, fish sauce, chilli sauce, sugar, sesame oil and garlic in a small bowl and mix together.

2 Heat the olive oil in a chargrill pan. Add the tuna steaks and cook over high heat for 2 minutes on each side, or until cooked to your liking. Transfer the steaks to a warm plate, cover and keep warm.

3 Place the noodles in a large saucepan of lightly salted, rapidly boiling water and return to the boil. Cook for 4 minutes, or until the noodles are tender. Drain well. Add half the dressing and half the spring onion and coriander to the noodles and gently toss together.

4 Either cut the tuna into even cubes or slice it.

5 Place the noodles on serving plates and top with the tuna. Mix the remaining dressing with the spring onion and coriander and drizzle over the tuna. Garnish with coriander leaves.

NUTRITION PER SERVE
Protein 32 g; Fat 10 g; Carbohydrate 5 g; Dietary Fibre 1 g; Cholesterol 105 mg; 1030 kJ (245 Cal)

Cook the tuna steaks in a chargrill pan until cooked to your liking.

Cook the noodles in l ghtly salted water until they are tender.

Fish burgers with tartare sauce

PREPARATION TIME: 30 MINUTES + 1 HOUR REFRIGERATION | TOTAL COOKING TIME: 25 MINUTES | SERVES 4

500 g (1 lb 2 oz) white fish fillets
2 tablespoons finely chopped parsley
2 tablespoons finely chopped dill
2 tablespoons lemon juice
1 tablespoon capers, drained and well rinsed and finely chopped
2 finely chopped gherkins (pickles)
350 g (12 oz) potatoes, cooked and mashed
plain (all-purpose) flour, for dusting
2 teaspoons olive oil
4 hamburger buns
lettuce leaves
2 roma (plum) tomatoes, sliced

TARTARE SAUCE
90 g (3¼ oz/⅓ cup) low-fat mayonnaise
½ finely chopped gherkin (pickle)
2 teaspoons capers, finely chopped
½ teaspoon malt vinegar
2 teaspoons finely chopped parsley
2 teaspoons lemon juice

1 Place the fish fillets in a frying pan and just cover with water. Slowly heat the water, making sure it doesn't boil. Cover and cook over low heat for 6–8 minutes, or until the fish is just cooked. Drain the fish on paper towels, transfer to a large bowl and flake with a fork. Add the parsley, dill, lemon juice, capers, gherkin and mashed potato, season well and mix thoroughly. Divide into four portions and shape into patties, handling the mixture carefully as it is quite soft. Dust lightly with flour and refrigerate on a plate for 1 hour.

2 Meanwhile, make the tartare sauce by mixing all the ingredients thoroughly in a bowl.

3 Heat the olive oil in a large non-stick frying pan, carefully add the patties and cook for 5–6 minutes on each side, or until well browned and heated through.

4 Meanwhile, cut the hamburger buns in half and toast under a grill (broiler). Fill the buns with lettuce leaves, tomato slices, the patties and then a spoonful of tartare sauce.

NUTRITION PER SERVE
Protein 40 g; Fat 15 g; Carbohydrate 70 g; Dietary Fibre 7 g; Cholesterol 95 mg; 2375 kJ (565 Cal)

Pour in enough water to cover the fish fillets and slowly heat the water.

Mix the flaked fish with the herbs, lemon juice, capers, gherkin, potato and seasoning.

Japanese-style salmon parcels

PREPARATION TIME: 40 MINUTES | TOTAL COOKING TIME: 15 MINUTES | SERVES 4

2 teaspoons sesame seeds
4 x 150 g (5½ oz) salmon cutlets or steaks
2.5 cm (1 inch) piece fresh ginger
2 celery stalks
4 spring onions (scallions)
¼ teaspoon dashi granules
3 tablespoons mirin
2 tablespoons tamari

1 Cut four squares of baking paper large enough to enclose the salmon steaks. Preheat the oven to 230°C (450°F/Gas 8). Lightly toast the sesame seeds under a hot grill (broiler) for 1 minute.

2 Wash the salmon and dry with paper towels. Place a salmon cutlet in the centre of each baking paper square.

3 Cut the ginger into paper-thin slices. Slice the celery and spring onions into short lengths, then lengthways into fine strips. Arrange a bundle of celery and spring onion and several slices of ginger on each salmon steak.

4 Combine the dashi granules, mirin and tamari in a small saucepan. Heat gently until the granules dissolve. Drizzle over each parcel, sprinkle with sesame seeds and carefully wrap the salmon, folding in the sides to seal in all the juices. Arrange the parcels on a baking tray and cook for about 12 minutes, or until tender. (The paper will puff up when the fish is cooked.) Do not overcook or the salmon will dry out. Serve immediately, as standing time can spoil the fish.

NOTE: *Dashi, mirin and tamari are all available from Asian food stores.*

Arrange celery and spring onion strips on the fish and top with ginger slices.

Wrap the salmon in baking paper, folding the sides to seal in the juices.

NUTRITION PER SERVE
Protein 20 g; Fat 14 g; Carbohydrate 0 g; Dietary Fibre 0.5 g; Cholesterol 85 mg; 935 kJ (225 Cal)

Tuna with chilli spiced mango sauce

PREPARATION TIME: 35 MINUTES | TOTAL COOKING TIME: 25 MINUTES | SERVES 4

1 large ripe mango
1 tablespoon oil
1 red onion, finely sliced
3 garlic cloves, finely chopped
4 cm (1½ inch) piece fresh ginger, finely chopped
2–3 red chillies, seeded and chopped
1 tablespoon honey
¼ teaspoon ground cinnamon
pinch ground cardamom
pinch ground nutmeg
pinch ground cloves
3 tablespoons dark rum
3 tablespoons lime juice
1 handful coriander (cilantro) leaves, chopped
cooking oil spray
4 tuna steaks

1 Peel the mango and dice the flesh. Heat the oil in a frying pan and add the onion, garlic, ginger and chilli. Cook for 3 minutes, or until the onion is soft.

2 Add the mango, honey, cinnamon, cardamom, nutmeg and cloves. Mix well and bring to the boil. Simmer gently for 5 minutes. Add the rum and simmer for a further 5 minutes. Add the lime juice and coriander and season.

3 Lightly spray a chargrill pan and cook the tuna for 2 minutes on each side. Serve with the sauce.

Peel the large ripe mango and cut the flesh into small cubes.

Fry the onion, garlic, ginger and chilli until the onion is soft.

NUTRITION PER SERVE
Protein 27 g; Fat 8 g; Carbohydrate 19 g; Dietary Fibre 3 g; Cholesterol 45 mg; 1200 kJ (300 Cal)

Crab curry

PREPARATION TIME: 25 MINUTES | TOTAL COOKING TIME: 20 MINUTES | SERVES 6

4 raw large blue swimmer or mud crabs
1 tablespoon oil
1 large onion, finely chopped
2 garlic cloves, crushed
1 lemongrass stem, white part only, finely chopped
1 teaspoon sambal oelek (South-East Asian chilli paste)
1 teaspoon ground cumin
1 teaspoon ground turmeric
1 teaspoon ground coriander
270 ml (9½ fl oz) light coconut cream
500 ml (17 fl oz/2 cups) chicken stock
1 large handful basil leaves

1 Pull back the apron and remove the top shell from the crabs. Remove the intestines and grey feathery gills. Cut each crab into four pieces. Use a cracker to crack the claws open; this will make it easier to eat later and will also allow the flavours to get into the crabmeat.

2 Heat the oil in a large saucepan or wok. Add the onion, garlic, lemongrass and sambal oelek and cook for 2–3 minutes, or until softened.

3 Add the cumin, turmeric, coriander and ½ teaspoon salt, and cook for a further 2 minutes, or until fragrant.

4 Stir in the coconut cream and stock. Bring to the boil, then reduce the heat, add the crab pieces and cook, stirring occasionally, for 10 minutes, or until the liquid has reduced and thickened slightly and the crabs are cooked through. Stir in the basil and serve with steamed rice.

NUTRITION PER SERVE
Protein 0.5 g; Fat 7 g; Carbohydrate 1.5 g; Dietary Fibre 0.5 g; Cholesterol 20 mg; 290 kJ (70 Cal)

Pull back the apron and remove the top shell from the crab.

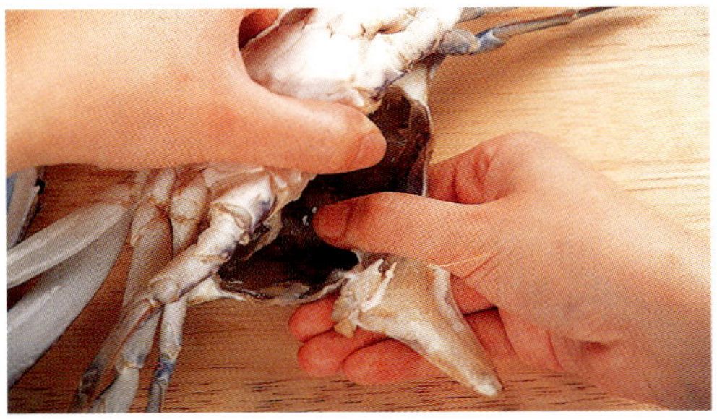

Remove the intestines and grey feathery gills from the crab.

Crack the claws open to allow the flavours to get into the crabmeat while it is cooking.

Tuna with lime and chilli sauce

PREPARATION TIME: 15 MINUTES | TOTAL COOKING TIME: 5 MINUTES | SERVES 4

2 large handfuls mint leaves, chopped
2 large handfuls coriander (cilantro) leaves, chopped, plus extra, to garnish
1 teaspoon grated lime zest
1 tablespoon lime juice
1 teaspoon grated fresh ginger
1 jalapeño chilli (pepper), seeded and finely chopped
250 g (9 oz/1 cup) low-fat natural yoghurt
4 tuna steaks

1 Mix together the mint, coriander, lime zest, lime juice, ginger and chilli. Fold in the yoghurt and season.

2 Cook the tuna in a lightly oiled chargrill pan for 2 minutes on each side. Serve with the sauce and garnish with coriander leaves.

NOTE: *Jalapeño chillies are smooth and thick-fleshed and are available as both red and green. They are quite fiery and you can use a less powerful variety of chilli if you prefer.*

NUTRITION PER SERVE
Protein 28 g; Fat 5 g; Carbohydrate 4 g; Dietary Fibre 1 g; Cholesterol 55 mg; 800 kJ (200 Cal)

It's a good idea to wear gloves to remove the seeds from chillies, to prevent skin irritation.

Mix together the mint, coriander, lime zest and juice, ginger and chilli.

Check the taste of the sauce before seasoning with salt and black pepper.

Crab, chilli and coriander noodles

PREPARATION TIME: 15 MINUTES | TOTAL COOKING TIME: 10 MINUTES | SERVES 4

1 tablespoon oil
4 spring onions (scallions), finely sliced
3 garlic cloves, crushed
2 green chillies, seeded and finely sliced
400 g (14 oz) fresh crabmeat
3 tablespoons lime juice
3 teaspoons grated lime zest
1 teaspoon caster (superfine) sugar
2 teaspoons sambal oelek (South-East Asian chilli paste)
375 g (13 oz) thin dried egg noodles
1 teaspoon sesame oil
2 tablespoons sweet chilli sauce
4 tablespoons chopped coriander (cilantro)

1 Heat the oil in a large frying pan and add the spring onion, garlic and chilli. Cook for 1–2 minutes over low heat, until soft. Add the crabmeat, lime juice and zest, caster sugar and sambal oelek. Stir until heated through and season to taste with salt.

2 Cook the noodles in boiling salted water for 2–3 minutes until tender. Drain well and toss with sesame oil.

3 Add the crab mixture, sweet chilli sauce and coriander to the noodles and gently toss. Serve immediately.

NOTE: *You can also use tinned crabmeat instead of fresh, but you will need 4 x 200 g (7 oz) tins, as a lot of weight will be lost when the meat is drained.*

Add the crabmeat, lime juice and zest, caster sugar and sambal oelek to the frying pan.

Cook the egg noodles in a large saucepan of boiling salted water.

NUTRITION PER SERVE
Protein 25 g; Fat 12 g; Carbohydrate 75 g; Dietary Fibre 5 g; Cholesterol 100 mg; 2340 kJ (560 Cal)

Spaghetti marinara

PREPARATION TIME: 50 MINUTES | TOTAL COOKING TIME: 30 MINUTES | SERVES 4

2 teaspoons olive oil
1 onion, chopped
2 garlic cloves, crushed
125 ml (4 fl oz/½ cup) dry red wine
2 tablespoons tomato paste (concentrated purée)
425 g (15 oz) tin chopped tomatoes
250 ml (9 fl oz/1 cup) bottled tomato pasta sauce
1 tablespoon each of chopped basil and oregano
12 mussels, hairy beards removed, and scrubbed
30 g (1 oz) butter
125 g (4½ oz) small squid tubes, cleaned and sliced
125 g (4½ oz) boneless firm white fish fillets, cubed
200 g (7 oz) raw prawns (shrimp), peeled and deveined, tails intact
500 g (1 lb 2 oz) spaghetti

1 Heat the olive oil in a large pan. Add the onion and garlic and cook over low heat for 2–3 minutes. Increase the heat to medium and add the wine, tomato paste, tomato and pasta sauce. Simmer, stirring occasionally, for 5–10 minutes or until the sauce reduces and thickens slightly. Stir in the herbs and season to taste. Keep warm.

2 While the sauce is simmering, heat 125 ml (4 fl oz/½ cup) water in a saucepan. Discard any broken mussels, or open ones that don't close when tapped on the work surface. Rinse well. Add the mussels. Cover and steam for 3–5 minutes, or until the mussels have opened and changed colour. Remove from the pan. Discard any unopened mussels. Stir the liquid into the tomato sauce.

3 Heat the butter in a frying pan and sauté the squid, fish and prawns, in batches, for 1–2 minutes, or until cooked. Add the seafood to the warm tomato sauce and stir gently.

4 Cook the pasta in a large saucepan of rapidly boiling salted water until *al dente* and then drain. Toss the seafood sauce with the pasta.

NUTRITION PER SERVE:
Protein 40 g; Fat 10 g; Carbohydrate 100 g; Dietary Fibre 10 g; Cholesterol 205 mg; 2840 kJ (675 Cal)

Pull the hairy beards away from the mussels and scrub the shells to remove any dirt or grit.

Remove the quills from inside the squid tubes and slice the tubes into thin rings.

Tuna kebabs

PREPARATION TIME: 20 MINUTES | TOTAL COOKING TIME: 20 MINUTES | SERVES 4

1 tablespoon olive oil
2–3 small red chillies, seeded and finely chopped
3–4 garlic cloves, crushed
1 red onion, finely chopped
3 tomatoes, seeded and chopped
3 tablespoons dry white wine or water
2 x 300 g (10½ oz) tins chickpeas, drained and rinsed
1 small handful oregano, chopped
1 very large handful parsley, chopped

TUNA KEBABS

1 kg (2 lb 4 oz) tuna fillet, cut into 4 cm (1½ inch) cubes
8 rosemary stalks, about 20 cm (8 inches) long, with leaves
cooking oil spray
lemon wedges, to serve

1 Heat the oil in a large frying pan, add the chilli, garlic and red onion and stir for 5 minutes, or until softened. Add the tomato and wine or water. Cook over low heat for 10 minutes, or until the mixture is soft, pulpy and the liquid has evaporated. Stir in the chickpeas, oregano and parsley. Season with salt and pepper.

2 Heat a barbeque grill plate or flat plate. Thread the tuna onto the rosemary stalks, lightly spray with oil, then cook, turning, for 3 minutes. Do not overcook or the tuna will fall apart. Serve with the chickpeas and lemon.

Stir the chopped chilli, crushed garlic and onion until softened.

Thread the tuna pieces onto the long rosemary stalks and grill or barbecue.

NUTRITION PER SERVE
Protein 75 g; Fat 15 g; Carbohydrate 25 g; Dietary Fibre 10 g; Cholesterol 110 mg; 2355 kJ (565 Cal)

Steamed trout with ginger and coriander

PREPARATION TIME: 20 MINUTES | TOTAL COOKING TIME: 30 MINUTES | SERVES 2

2 whole rainbow trout (about 320 g/ 11¼ oz each), cleaned and scaled
2 limes, thinly sliced
5 cm (2 inch) piece fresh ginger, cut into matchsticks
60 g (2¼ oz/¼ cup) caster (superfine) sugar
60 ml (2 fl oz/¼ cup) lime juice
zest of 1 lime, cut into thin strips
1 large handful coriander (cilantro) leaves

1 Preheat the oven to 180°C (350°F/Gas 4). Fill the fish cavities with the lime slices and some of the ginger, then place the fish on a large piece of greased foil. Wrap the fish and bake on a baking tray for 20–30 minutes, until the flesh flakes easily when tested with a fork.

2 Meanwhile, combine the sugar and lime juice with 250 ml (9 fl oz) water in a small saucepan and stir without boiling until the sugar dissolves. Bring to the boil, reduce the heat and simmer for 10 minutes, or until syrupy. Stir in the remaining ginger and lime zest. Put the fish on a plate. Top with coriander leaves and pour the hot syrup over it.

NUTRITION PER SERVE
Protein 50 g; Fat 10 g; Carbohydrate 30 g; Dietary Fibre 1 g; Cholesterol 120 mg; 1715 kJ (410 Cal)

Peel the fresh ginger with a potato peeler and cut it into fine, short matchsticks.

Fill the cavities of the trout with the lime slices and some of the ginger.

Simmer the sugar, lime juice and water until you have a syrupy sauce.

Vegetarian

Potato gnocchi with tomato sauce

PREPARATION TIME: 1 HOUR | TOTAL COOKING TIME: 45 MINUTES | SERVES 4

500 g (1 lb 2 oz) floury potatoes, unpeeled
1 egg yolk
3 tablespoons grated parmesan cheese, plus extra, to serve
125 g (4½ oz/1 cup) plain (all-purpose) flour

TOMATO SAUCE
425 g (15 oz) tin tomatoes, chopped
1 small onion, chopped
1 celery stalk, chopped
1 small carrot, chopped
1 tablespoon shredded basil
1 teaspoon chopped thyme
1 garlic clove, crushed
1 teaspoon caster (superfine) sugar

NUTRITION PER SERVE
Protein 10 g; Fat 4 g; Carbohydrate 45 g; Dietary Fibre 5 g; Cholesterol 50 mg; 1125 kJ (270 Cal)

1 Steam or boil the potatoes until just tender. Drain thoroughly and allow to cool for 10 minutes before peeling and mashing them.

2 Measure 2 cups of the mashed potato into a large bowl, mix in the egg yolk, parmesan, ¼ teaspoon of salt and some black pepper. Slowly add flour until you have a slightly sticky dough. Knead for 5 minutes, adding more flour if necessary, until a smooth dough is formed.

3 Divide the dough into four portions and roll each portion on a lightly floured surface to form a sausage shape, about 2 cm (¾ inch) thick.

4 Cut the rolls into 2.5 cm (1 inch) slices and shape each piece into an oval. Press each oval into the palm of your hand against a floured fork, to flatten slightly and indent one side with a pattern. As you make the gnocchi place them in a single layer on a baking tray and cover until ready to use.

5 To make the tomato sauce, mix all the ingredients with salt and pepper in a saucepan. Bring to the boil, reduce the heat to low–medium and simmer for 30 minutes, stirring occasionally. Allow to cool, then process in a food processor or blender, until smooth. Reheat if necessary before serving.

6 Cook the gnocchi in batches in a large saucepan of boiling salted water for 2 minutes, or until the gnocchi float to the surface. Drain well. Serve the gnocchi tossed through the sauce, sprinkled with parmesan.

Roll each portion into a sausage shape, on a lightly floured surface.

Press each oval with a floured fork to flatten slightly and make an indentation.

Cook the gnocchi in a large saucepan of boiling water until they float to the surface.

Stuffed eggplants

PREPARATION TIME: 20 MINUTES | TOTAL COOKING TIME: 1 HOUR | SERVES 4

60 g (2¼ oz/⅓ cup) brown lentils
2 large eggplants (aubergines)
cooking oil spray
1 red onion, chopped
2 garlic cloves, crushed
1 red capsicum (pepper), finely chopped
40 g (1½ oz/¼ cup) pine nuts, toasted
140 g (5 oz/¾ cup) cooked short-grain rice
440 g (15½ oz) tin chopped tomatoes
2 tablespoons chopped coriander (cilantro)
1 tablespoon chopped parsley
2 tablespoons grated parmesan cheese

1 Simmer the brown lentils in a saucepan of water for 25 minutes, or until soft; drain. Slice the eggplants in half lengthways and scoop out the flesh, leaving a 1 cm (½ inch) shell. Chop the flesh finely.

2 Spray a large, deep non-stick frying pan with oil, add 1 tablespoon water to the pan, then add the onion and garlic and stir until softened. Add the cooked lentils to the pan with the capsicum, pine nuts, rice, tomato and eggplant flesh. Stir over medium heat for 10 minutes, or until the eggplant has softened. Add the fresh coriander and parsley. Season, then toss until well mixed.

3 Cook the eggplant shells in boiling water for 4–5 minutes, or until tender. Spoon the filling into the eggplant shells and sprinkle with the parmesan. Grill (broil) for 5–10 minutes, or until golden. Serve immediately.

Scoop out the flesh, leaving a shell on the inside of the eggplant halves.

Stir in the chopped fresh coriander and parsley and season.

NUTRITION PER SERVE

Protein 15 g; Fat 10 g; Carbohydrate 50 g; Dietary Fibre 8.5 g; Cholesterol 9.5 mg; 1490 kJ (355 Cal)

Vegetable curry

PREPARATION TIME: 20 MINUTES | TOTAL COOKING TIME: 30 MINUTES | SERVES 6

250 g (9 oz) potatoes, peeled and diced
250 g (9 oz) pumpkin (winter squash), peeled and diced
200 g (7 oz) cauliflower, broken into florets
150 g (5½ oz) yellow squash, cut into quarters
1 tablespoon oil
2 onions, chopped
3 tablespoons curry powder
400 g (14 oz) tin chopped tomatoes
250 ml (9 fl oz/1 cup) vegetable stock
150 g (5½ oz) green beans, cut into short lengths
90 g (3¼ oz/⅓ cup) plain low-fat yoghurt
30 g (1 oz/¼ cup) sultanas (golden raisins)

1 Bring a saucepan of water to the boil, add the potato and pumpkin, and cook for 6 minutes, then remove. Add the cauliflower and squash, cook for 4 minutes, then remove.

2 Heat the oil in a large saucepan, add the onion and cook, stirring, over medium heat for 8 minutes, or until starting to brown.

3 Add the curry powder and stir for 1 minute, or until fragrant. Stir in the tomato and stock.

4 Add the parboiled potato, pumpkin, cauliflower and squash and cook for 5 minutes, then add the green beans and cook for a further 2–3 minutes, or until the vegetables are just tender.

5 Add the yoghurt and sultanas, and stir to combine. Simmer for 3 minutes, or until thickened slightly. Season to taste and serve.

Cook the onion over medium heat until it is starting to brown.

Add the beans and cook until the vegetables are just tender.

NUTRITION PER SERVE
Protein 7 g; Fat 8.5 g; Carbohydrate 20 g; Dietary Fibre 7 g; Cholesterol 2.5 mg; 805 kJ (192 Cal)

Polenta pie

PREPARATION TIME: 20 MINUTES + 15 MINUTES STANDING + REFRIGERATION | TOTAL COOKING TIME: 50 MINUTES | SERVES 6

2 eggplants (aubergines), thickly sliced
330 ml (11¼ fl oz/1⅓ cups) vegetable stock
150 g (5½ oz/1 cup) fine polenta
60 g (2¼ oz/heaped ½ cup) finely grated parmesan cheese
1 tablespoon olive oil
1 large onion, chopped
2 garlic cloves, crushed
1 large red capsicum (pepper), diced
2 zucchini (courgettes), thickly sliced
150 g (5½ oz) button mushrooms, cut into quarters
400 g (14 oz) tin chopped tomatoes
3 teaspoons balsamic vinegar
olive oil, for brushing

NUTRITION PER SERVE
Protein 8 g; Fat 8.5 g; Carbohydrate 23 g; Dietary Fibre 4.5 g; Cholesterol 8 mg; 855 kJ (205 Cal)

1 Spread the eggplant in a single layer on a board and sprinkle with salt. Leave for 15 minutes, then rinse, pat dry and cut into cubes.

2 Line a 23 cm (9 inch) round cake tin with foil. Pour the stock and 330 ml (11¼ fl oz/1⅓ cups) water into a saucepan and bring to the boil. Add the polenta in a thin stream and stir over low heat for 5 minutes, or until the liquid is absorbed and the mixture comes away from the side of the pan.

3 Remove from the heat and stir in the cheese until it melts through the polenta. Spread into the prepared tin, smoothing the surface as much as possible. Refrigerate until set.

4 Preheat the oven to 200°C (400°F/Gas 6). Heat the oil in a large saucepan with a lid and add the onion. Cook over medium heat, stirring occasionally, for about 3 minutes. Add the garlic and cook for a further minute. Add the eggplant, capsicum, zucchini, mushrooms and tomato. Bring to the boil, then reduce the heat and simmer, covered, for about 20 minutes. Stir occasionally to prevent it catching on the bottom of the pan. Stir in the vinegar and season.

5 Transfer the vegetable mixture to a 23 cm (9 inch) ovenproof pie dish, piling it up slightly in the centre. Turn out the polenta, peel off the foil and cut into 12 wedges. Arrange smooth side down in a single layer, over the vegetables Brush lightly with a little olive oil and bake for 20 minutes, or until lightly brown and crisp.

Cook the polenta, stirring, until all the liquid is absorbed and it is very thick.

Reduce the heat and simmer until the vegetables are tender.

Arrange the polenta wedges, smooth side down, over the vegetable mixture—don't worry about gaps.

Pumpkin and broad bean risotto

PREPARATION TIME: 35 MINUTES | TOTAL COOKING TIME: 50 MINUTES | SERVES 4

350 g (12 oz) pumpkin (winter squash)
cooking oil spray
1 tablespoon olive oil
1 large onion, finely chopped
2 garlic cloves, finely chopped
750 ml (26 fl oz/3 cups) vegetable stock
220 g (7¾ oz/1 cup) arborio rice
200 g (7 oz) Swiss brown mushrooms, halved
310 g (11 oz/2 cups) frozen broad (fava) beans, defrosted, peeled
4 tablespoons grated parmesan cheese (optional)

1 Preheat the oven to moderately hot 200°C (400°F/Gas 6). Cut the pumpkin into small chunks, place on a baking tray and spray lightly with oil. Bake, turning occasionally, for 20 minutes, or until tender. Set aside, covered.

2 Meanwhile, heat the oil in a large heavy-based saucepan, add the onion and garlic, cover and cook for 10 minutes over low heat. Put the stock in a different saucepan and keep at simmering point on the stovetop.

3 Add the rice to the onion and stir for 2 minutes. Gradually stir in 125 ml (4 fl oz/½ cup) of the hot stock, until absorbed. Stir in another 125 ml (4 fl oz/½ cup) of hot stock until absorbed. Add the mushrooms and continue adding the remaining stock, a little at a time, until it is all absorbed and the rice is just tender (this will take about 25 minutes).

4 Stir in the cooked pumpkin and the broad beans. Sprinkle with the grated parmesan, if desired.

Put the chunks of pumpkin on a baking tray and spray with oil.

Add the stock to the rice, a little at a time, and stir until absorbed.

NUTRITION PER SERVE
Protein 20 g; Fat 12 g; Carbohydrate 60 g; Dietary Fibre 10 g; Cholesterol 20 mg; 1775 kJ (425 Cal)

Summer potato pizza

PREPARATION TIME: 30 MINUTES | TOTAL COOKING TIME: 40 MINUTES | SERVES 6

10 g (¼ oz) sachet dry yeast
310 g (11 oz/2½ cups) plain (all-purpose) flour
2 teaspoons polenta or semolina
2 tablespoons olive oil
2 garlic cloves, crushed
4–5 potatoes, unpeeled, thinly sliced
1 tablespoon rosemary leaves

1 Preheat the oven to 210°C (415°F/Gas 6–7). Combine the yeast, ½ teaspoon of salt and sugar and 250 ml (9 fl oz/1 cup) of warm water in a bowl. Cover and leave in a warm place for 10 minutes, or until foamy. Sift the flour into a bowl, make a well in the centre, add the yeast mixture and mix to a dough.

2 Turn the dough out onto a lightly floured surface and knead for 5 minutes, or until smooth and elastic. Roll out to a 30 cm (12 inch) circle. Lightly spray a pizza tray with oil and sprinkle with the polenta or semolina.

3 Place the pizza base on the tray. Mix 2 teaspoons of the oil with the garlic and brush over the pizza base. Gently toss the remaining olive oil, potato slices, rosemary leaves, 1 teaspoon of salt and some pepper in a bowl.

4 Arrange the potato slices in overlapping circles over the pizza base and bake for 40 minutes, or until the base is crisp and golden.

Leave the yeast mixture in a warm place until it becomes foamy—this shows it is active.

Brush the dough base with garlic oil, then top with a layer of potato slices.

NUTRITION PER SERVE

Protein 9 g; Fat 10 g; Carbohydrate 50 g; Dietary Fibre 4 g; Cholesterol 0 mg; 1415 kJ (340 Cal)

Red lentil and ricotta lasagne

PREPARATION TIME: 30 MINUTES + SOAKING | TOTAL COOKING TIME: 2 HOURS 10 MINUTES | SERVES 6

125 g (4½ oz/½ cup) red lentils
2 teaspoons olive oil
2–3 garlic cloves, crushed
1 large onion, chopped
1 small red capsicum (pepper), chopped
2 zucchini (courgettes), sliced
1 celery stalk, sliced
2 x 425 g (15 oz) tins chopped tomatoes
2 tablespoons tomato paste (concentrated purée)
1 teaspoon dried oregano
350 g (12 oz) ricotta cheese
12 dried or fresh lasagne sheets
60 g (2¼ oz/½ cup) low-fat cheddar cheese, grated

WHITE SAUCE
40 g (1½ oz/⅓ cup) cornflour (cornstarch)
750 ml (26 fl oz/3 cups) skim milk
¼ onion
½ teaspoon ground nutmeg

NUTRITION PER SERVE
Protein 25 g; Fat 10 g; Carbohydrate 65 g; Dietary Fibre 9 g; Cholesterol 40 mg; 1995 kJ (475 Cal)

1 Soak the lentils in boiling water to cover for at least 30 minutes, then drain. Meanwhile, heat the oil in a large pan, add the garlic and onion and cook for 2 minutes. Add the capsicum, zucchini and celery and cook for 2–3 minutes.

2 Add the lentils, tomato, tomato paste, oregano and 375 ml (13 fl oz/1½ cups) water. Bring slowly to the boil, reduce the heat and simmer for 30 minutes, or until the lentils are tender. Stir occasionally.

3 To make the white sauce, blend the cornflour with 2 tablespoons of the milk in a saucepan until smooth. Pour the remaining milk into the pan, add the onion and stir over low heat until the mixture boils and thickens. Add the nutmeg and season with pepper, then cook over low heat for 5 minutes. Remove the onion.

4 Beat the ricotta with about 125 ml (4 fl oz/½ cup) of the white sauce. Preheat the oven to moderate 180°C (350°F/Gas 4). Spread one-third of the lentil mixture over the base of a 3 litre (105 fl oz/12 cup) capacity ovenproof dish. Cover with a layer of lasagne sheets. Spread another third of the lentil mixture over the pasta, then spread the ricotta evenly over the top. Follow with another layer of lasagne, then the remaining lentils. Pour the white sauce evenly over the top and sprinkle with the grated cheese. Bake for 1 hour, covering loosely with foil if the top starts to brown too much. Leave to stand for 5 minutes before cutting.

Chop the onion and capsicum into quite small pieces and slice the zucchini.

Build up layers of the lentil mixture, lasagne sheets and ricotta.

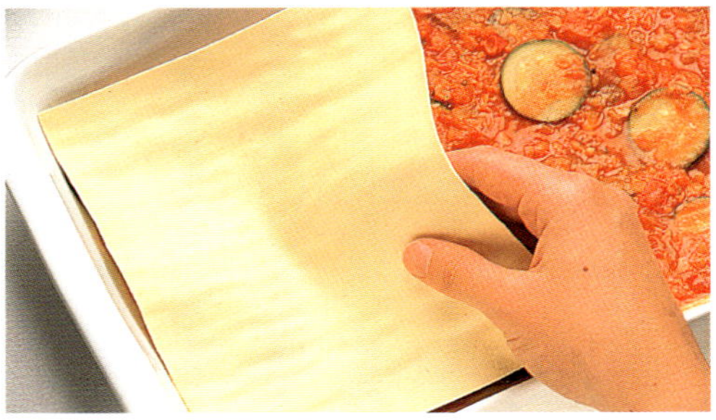

Pour the white sauce evenly over the top of the lasagne, then sprinkle with cheese.

Vegetarian chilli

PREPARATION TIME: 15 MINUTES | TOTAL COOKING TIME: 40 MINUTES | SERVES 8

150 g (5½ oz/¾ cup) burghul (bulgur)
1 tablespoon olive oil
1 large onion, finely chopped
2 garlic cloves, crushed
1 teaspoon chilli powder
2 teaspoons ground cumin
1 teaspoon cayenne pepper
½ teaspoon ground cinnamon
2 x 400 g (14 oz) tins chopped tomatoes
750 ml (26 fl oz/3 cups) vegetable stock
440 g (15½ oz) tin red kidney beans, drained and rinsed
2 x 300 g (10½ oz) tins chickpeas, drained and rinsed
310 g (11 oz) tin corn kernels, drained
2 tablespoons tomato paste (concentrated purée)
corn chips and light sour cream, for serving

1 Soak the burghul in 250 ml (9 fl oz/1 cup) hot water for 10 minutes. Heat the oil in a large heavy-based saucepan and cook the onion for 10 minutes, stirring often, until soft and golden.

2 Add the garlic, chilli powder, cumin, cayenne and cinnamon and cook, stirring, for a further minute.

3 Add the tomato, stock and burghul. Bring to the boil and simmer for 10 minutes. Stir in the beans, chickpeas, corn and tomato paste and simmer for 20 minutes, stirring often. Serve with corn chips and sour cream.

STORAGE TIME: *Chilli will keep for up to 3 days in the refrigerator (and can be frozen for up to 1 month).*

Stir the garlic and spices into the pan with the onion and cook for a minute.

Add the kidney beans, chickpeas, corn and tomato paste to the pan.

NUTRITION PER SERVE
Protein 7 g; Fat 10 g; Carbohydrate 18 g; Dietary Fibre 7 g; Cholesterol 8 mg; 780 kJ (185 Cal)

Pasta napolitana

PREPARATION TIME: 20 MINUTES | TOTAL COOKING TIME: 1 HOUR | SERVES 6

1 tablespoon olive oil
1 onion, finely chopped
1 carrot, finely chopped
1 celery stalk, finely chopped
500 g (1 lb 2 oz) ripe tomatoes, chopped
2 tablespoons chopped parsley
2 teaspoons sugar
500 g (1 lb 2 oz) pasta (see NOTE)

1 Heat the oil in a heavy-based saucepan. Add the onion, carrot and celery. Cover and cook for 10 minutes over low heat, stirring occasionally.

2 Add the tomato to the vegetables with the parsley, sugar and 125 ml (4 fl oz/½ cup) water. Bring to the boil, reduce the heat to low, cover and simmer for 45 minutes, stirring occasionally. Season with salt and pepper. If necessary, add a little more water to thin the sauce.

3 Add the pasta to a large saucepan of rapidly boiling salted water and cook until *al dente*. Drain and return to the pan. Pour the sauce over the pasta and gently toss.

NOTE: *Traditionally, spaghetti is used with this sauce, but you can use any pasta. The sauce can be reduced to a concentrated version by cooking it for a longer period. Store it in the refrigerator and add water or stock to thin it, if necessary, when reheating.*

Chop the vegetables into small even pieces before adding to the oil.

Add the chopped tomatoes, parsley, sugar and water to the cooked vegetables.

NUTRITION PER SERVE
Protein 10 g; Fat 7 g; Carbohydrate 65 g; Dietary Fibre 6 g; Cholesterol 0 mg; 1540 kJ (365 Cal)

GEORGES
DUBŒUF

Vegetable casserole with herb dumplings

PREPARATION TIME: 30 MINUTES | TOTAL COOKING TIME: 50 MINUTES | SERVES 4

1 tablespoon olive oil
1 large onion, chopped
2 garlic cloves, crushed
2 teaspoons sweet paprika
1 large potato, chopped
1 large carrot, sliced
400 g (14 oz) tin chopped tomatoes
375 ml (13 fl oz/1½ cups) vegetable stock
400 g (14 oz) orange sweet potato, cubed
150 g (5½ oz) broccoli, cut into florets
2 zucchini (courgettes), thickly sliced
125 g (4½ oz/1 cup) self-raising flour
20 g (¾ oz) cold butter, cut into small cubes
2 teaspoons chopped parsley
1 teaspoon thyme
1 teaspoon chopped rosemary
4 tablespoons milk
2 tablespoons light sour cream

NUTRITION PER SERVE
Protein 8 g; Fat 10 g; Carbohydrate 27 g; Dietary Fibre 7.5 g; Cholesterol 16 mg; 967 kJ (230 Cal)

1 Heat the oil in a large saucepan and add the onion. Cook over low heat, stirring occasionally, for 5 minutes, or until soft. Add the garlic and paprika and cook, stirring, for 1 minute.

2 Add the potato, carrot, tomato and stock to the pan. Bring to the boil, then reduce the heat and simmer, covered, for 10 minutes. Add the sweet potato, broccoli and zucchini and simmer for 10 minutes, or until tender. Preheat the oven to 200°C (400°F/Gas 6).

3 To make the dumplings, sift the flour and a pinch of salt into a bowl and add the butter. Rub the butter into the flour with your fingertips until it resembles fine breadcrumbs Stir in the herbs and make a well in the centre. Add the milk, and mix with a flat-bladed knife, using a cutting action, until the mixture comes together in beads. Gather up the dough and lift onto a lightly floured surface, then divide into eight portions. Shape each portion into a ball.

4 Add the sour cream to the casserole. Pour into a 2 litre (70 fl oz/8 cup) ovenproof dish and top with the dumplings. Bake for 20 minutes, or until the dumplings are golden and a skewer comes out clean when inserted in the centre.

Add the sweet potato, broccoli and zucchini and simmer for 10 minutes, or until they are tender.

Rub the butter into the flour until the mixture resembles fine breadcrumbs.

Divide the dough into eight equal portions and shape each portion into a dumpling.

Fettuccine boscaiola

PREPARATION TIME: 20 MINUTES | TOTAL COOKING TIME: 25 MINUTES | SERVES 6

500 g (1 lb 2 oz) button mushrooms
1 large onion
1 tablespoon olive oil
2 garlic cloves, finely chopped
2 x 425 g (15 oz) tins tomatoes, chopped
500 g (1 lb 2 oz) fettuccine
2 tablespoons chopped parsley

1 Wipe the mushrooms with a damp paper towel and then slice finely, including the stems.

2 Chop the onion roughly. Heat the oil in a heavy-based frying pan and cook the onion and garlic over medium heat, stirring occasionally, for about 6 minutes, or until the vegetables are light golden. Add the tomato including the juice, along with the mushrooms, to the pan and bring the mixture to the boil. Reduce the heat, cover the pan and simmer for 15 minutes.

3 While the sauce is cooking, cook the fettuccine in a large saucepan of rapidly boiling salted water until *al dente*. Drain and return to the pan.

4 Stir the parsley into the sauce and season well with salt and pepper. Toss the sauce through the pasta.

NUTRITION PER SERVE
Protein 15 g; Fat 10 g; Carbohydrate 65 g; Dietary Fibre 10 g; Cholesterol 0 mg; 1640 kJ (390 Cal)

Wipe the mushrooms with a damp paper towel to remove any dirt.

Use a large sharp knife to roughly chop the onion and then cook until golden.

Add the chopped tomatoes and sliced mushrooms to the frying pan.

Potatoes in Mediterranean sauce

PREPARATION TIME: 30 MINUTES | TOTAL COOKING TIME: 50 MINUTES | SERVES 6

1 kg (2 lb 4 oz) new or baby potatoes, unpeeled and halved
1 tablespoon olive oil
2 onions, finely chopped
3 garlic cloves, crushed
1 teaspoon sweet paprika
425 g (15 oz) tin chopped tomatoes
2 tablespoons lemon juice
½ teaspoon grated lemon zest
2 teaspoons soft brown sugar
3 teaspoons tomato paste (concentrated purée)
½ teaspoon dried thyme
12 kalamata olives
1 tablespoon capers, rinsed and roughly chopped
150 g (5½ oz) feta cheese, cubed
1 tablespoon roughly chopped parsley

1 Boil the potato until just tender. Heat the olive oil in a large saucepan, add the onion and cook until soft and golden. Add the garlic and paprika and cook for another minute.

2 Stir in the tomato, lemon juice, lemon zest, sugar, tomato paste and thyme. Simmer, covered, for 5 minutes and then add the potato and toss to coat. Simmer, covered, for 20 minutes, or until the potato is cooked through. Stir occasionally to prevent burning.

3 Remove the pan from the heat and, just before serving, stir through the olives, capers and feta. Season to taste and scatter the parsley over the top before serving.

NUTRITION PER SERVE
Protein 10 g; Fat 10 g; Carbohydrate 30 g; Dietary Fibre 5 g; Cholesterol 15 mg; 1120 kJ (270 Cal)

Stir in the tomato, lemon juice and zest, sugar, tomato paste and thyme.

Add the potato to the tomato sauce. Toss to coat well and then leave to simmer.

Mushroom, ricotta and olive pizza

PREPARATION TIME: 30 MINUTES + PROVING | TOTAL COOKING TIME: 1 HOUR | SERVES 6

4 roma (plum) tomatoes, quartered
¾ teaspoon caster (superfine) sugar
10 g (¼ oz) dry yeast or 15 g (½ oz) fresh yeast
125 ml (4 fl oz/½ cup) skim milk
220 g (7¾ oz/1¾ cups) plain (all-purpose) flour
2 teaspoons olive oil
2 garlic cloves, crushed
1 onion, thinly sliced
750 g (1 lb 10 oz) mushrooms, sliced
250 g (9 oz/1 cup) low-fat ricotta cheese
2 tablespoons sliced black olives
small handful basil leaves

NUTRITION PER SERVE
Protein 15 g; Fat 7.5 g; Carbohydrate 30g; Dietary Fibre 6 g; Cholesterol 20 mg; 1100 kJ (265 Cal)

1 Preheat the oven to 210°C (415°F/ Gas 6–7). Put the tomato on a baking tray covered with baking paper, sprinkle with salt, cracked black pepper and ½ teaspoon sugar and bake for 20 minutes, or until the edges are starting to darken.

2 Stir the yeast and remaining sugar with 3 tablespoons warm water until the yeast dissolves. Cover and leave in a warm place until foamy. Warm the milk. Sift the flour into a large bowl and stir in the yeast and milk. Mix to a soft dough, then turn onto a lightly floured surface and knead for 5 minutes. Leave, covered, in a lightly oiled bowl in a warm place for 40 minutes, or until doubled in size.

3 Heat the oil in a frying pan and fry the garlic and onion until soft. Add the mushrooms and stir until they are soft and the liquid has evaporated. Leave to cool.

4 Turn the dough out onto a lightly floured surface and knead lightly. Roll out to a 38 cm (15 inch) circle and transfer to a lightly greased oven or pizza tray. Spread with the ricotta, leaving a border to turn over the filling. Top with the mushrooms, leaving a circle in the centre, and arrange the tomato and olives in the circle. Fold the dough edge over onto the mushroom and dust the edge with flour. Bake for 25 minutes, or until the crust is golden. Garnish with basil.

The yeast mixture is ready when it starts to foam—this shows the yeast is active.

Spread the ricotta over the pastry, leaving a border to turn over the filling.

Middle Eastern potato casserole

PREPARATION TIME: 10 MINUTES | TOTAL COOKING TIME: 30 MINUTES | SERVES 4

¼ teaspoon saffron threads
1 kg (2 lb 4 oz) potatoes, cut into large cubes
1 teaspoon olive oil
1 small onion, sliced
½ teaspoon ground turmeric
½ teaspoon ground coriander
250 ml (9 fl oz/1 cup) vegetable stock
1 garlic clove, crushed
30 g (1 oz/¼ cup) raisins
1 teaspoon chopped parsley
1 teaspoon chopped coriander (cilantro) leaves

1 Put the saffron to soak in 1 tablespoon hot water. Place the potato in a saucepan of cold, salted water. Bring to the boil and cook for 12 minutes, or until tender but still firm. Drain and set aside.

2 Heat the oil in a separate saucepan, add the onion, turmeric and ground coriander and cook over low heat for 5 minutes, or until the onion is soft.

3 Add the potato, vegetable stock and garlic. Bring to the boil, then reduce the heat and simmer for 10 minutes.

4 Add the saffron with its soaking water and the raisins, and cook for 10 minutes, or until the potato is soft and the sauce has reduced and thickened. Stir in the parsley and coriander. Delicious with couscous.

Soak the saffron threads in 1 tablespoon hot water while you cook the potatoes.

Cook the onion, turmeric and ground coriander until the onion is soft.

NUTRITION PER SERVE
Protein 10 g; Fat 6 g; Carbohydrate 65 g; Dietary Fibre 8 g; Cholesterol 0.5 mg; 1500 kJ (358 Cal)

Silverbeet parcels

PREPARATION TIME: 40 MINUTES | TOTAL COOKING TIME: 1 HOUR | SERVES 6

500 ml (17 fl oz/2 cups) vegetable stock
1 tablespoon olive oil
1 onion, chopped
2 garlic cloves, crushed
1 red capsicum (pepper), chopped
250 g (9 oz) mushrooms, chopped
110 g (3¾ oz/½ cup) arborio rice
60 g (2¼ oz/1½ cups) low-fat cheddar cheese, grated
1 large handful shredded basil
6 large silverbeet (Swiss chard) leaves
2 x 400 g (14 oz) tins chopped tomatoes
1 tablespoon balsamic vinegar
1 teaspoon soft brown sugar

1 Heat the stock in a saucepan and maintain at simmering point. Heat the oil in a large saucepan, add the onion and garlic and cook until the onion has softened. Add the capsicum, mushrooms and rice and stir until well combined. Gradually add 125 ml (4 fl oz/ ½ cup) hot stock, stirring until the liquid has been absorbed. Continue to add the stock, a little at a time, until it has all been absorbed and the rice is tender. Remove from the heat, add the cheese and basil and season to taste.

2 Trim the stalks from the silverbeet and cook the leaves, a few at a time, in a large saucepan of boiling water for 30 seconds, or until wilted. Drain on a tea towel (dish towel). Using a sharp knife, cut away any tough white veins from the centre of the leaves. Place a portion of mushroom filling in the centre of each leaf, fold in the sides and roll up carefully. Tie with string.

3 Put the tomato, balsamic vinegar and sugar in a large, deep non-stick frying pan and stir to combine. Add the silverbeet parcels, cover and simmer for 10 minutes. Remove the string and serve with tomato sauce.

Using a sharp knife, cut away the white veins from the centre of the leaves.

Place the filling in the centre of each leaf, fold in the sides and roll up into parcels.

NUTRITION PER SERVE
Protein 7.5 g; Fat 6 g; Carbohydrate 20 g; Dietary Fibre 4 g; Cholesterol 7 mg; 725 kJ (175 Cal)

Roast vegetable quiche

PREPARATION TIME: 45 MINUTES + 25 MINUTES REFRIGERATION | TOTAL COOKING TIME: 2 HOURS 30 MINUTES | SERVES 6

cooking oil spray
1 large potato
400 g (14 oz) pumpkin (winter squash)
200 g (7 oz) orange sweet potato
2 large parsnips
1 red capsicum (pepper)
2 onions, cut into wedges
6 garlic cloves, halved
2 teaspoons olive oil
150 g (5½ oz/1¼ cups) plain (all-purpose) flour
40 g (1½ oz) butter
40 g (1½ oz) ricotta cheese
250 ml (9 fl oz/1 cup) skim milk
3 eggs, lightly beaten
30 g (1 oz/¼ cup) grated low-fat cheddar cheese
2 tablespoons chopped basil

NUTRITION PER SERVE
Protein 15 g; Fat 10 g; Carbohydrate 45 g; Dietary Fibre 5.5 g; Cholesterol 115 mg; 1440 kJ (345 Cal)

1 Preheat the oven to 180°C (350°F/Gas 4). Lightly spray a 3 cm (1¼ inch) deep, 23 cm (9 inch) diameter loose-based flan (tart) tin with oil. Cut the potato, pumpkin, sweet potato, parsnips and capsicum into bite-sized chunks, place in a baking dish with the onion and garlic and drizzle with the oil. Season and bake for 1 hour, or until the vegetables are tender. Leave to cool.

2 Mix the flour, butter and ricotta in a food processor, then gradually add up to 3 tablespoons of the milk, enough to form a soft dough. Turn out onto a lightly floured surface and gather together into a smooth ball. Cover and refrigerate for 15 minutes.

3 Roll the pastry out on a lightly floured surface, then ease into the tin, bringing it gently up the side. Trim the edge and refrigerate for another 10 minutes. Increase the oven to 200°C (400°F/Gas 6). Cover the pastry with crumpled baking paper and fill with baking beads or uncooked rice. Bake for 10 minutes, remove the beads or rice and paper, then bake for another 10 minutes, or until golden brown.

4 Place the vegetables in the pastry base and pour in the combined remaining milk, eggs, cheese and basil. Reduce the oven temperature to 180°C (350°F/Gas 4) and bake for 1 hour 10 minutes, or until set in the centre. Leave for 5 minutes before removing from the tin to serve.

Put the vegetables in a baking dish and drizzle with the olive oil.

Ease the pastry into the flan tin, bring it up the side, then trim the edge.

Mix the milk, eggs, cheese and basil and pour over the vegetables.

Frittata

PREPARATION TIME: 25 MINUTES | TOTAL COOKING TIME: 25 MINUTES | SERVES 6

200 g (7 oz) zucchini (courgettes), cubed
250 g (9 oz) pumpkin (winter squash), cubed
300 g (10½ oz) potato, cubed
100 g (3½ oz) broccoli florets
3 teaspoons oil
1 small onion, chopped
1 small red capsicum (pepper), chopped
2 tablespoons chopped parsley
3 eggs
2 egg whites

1 Steam the zucchini, pumpkin, potato and broccoli until tender.

2 Heat 2 teaspoons of the oil in a non-stick frying pan, about 23 cm (9 inch) diameter. Add the onion and capsicum and cook for 3 minutes, or until tender. Mix in a bowl with the steamed vegetables, along with the parsley.

3 Brush the pan with the remaining oil. Return all the vegetables to the pan and spread out with a spatula to an even thickness. Beat the eggs and whites together and pour into the pan.

4 Cook over medium heat until the eggs are almost set, but still runny on top. Wrap the handle of the pan in foil to protect it and place under a hot grill (broiler) to brown the frittata top (pierce gently with a fork to make sure it is cooked through). Cut into wedges to serve.

Beat the eggs and whites together and pour into the pan over the vegetables.

The eggs should be almost set, but still runny on top, before you put them under the grill.

NUTRITION PER SERVE
Protein 8 g; Fat 5 g; Carbohydrate 10 g; Dietary Fibre 3 g; Cholesterol 90 mg; 515 kJ (125 Cal)

Chickpea curry

PREPARATION TIME: 10 MINUTES + OVERNIGHT SOAKING | TOTAL COOKING TIME: 1 HOUR 15 MINUTES | SERVES 6

220 g (7¾ oz/1 cup) dried chickpeas
1 tablespoon oil
2 onions, finely chopped
2 large ripe tomatoes, chopped
½ teaspoon ground coriander
1 teaspoon ground cumin
1 teaspoon chilli powder
¼ teaspoon ground turmeric
1 tablespoon channa masala (see NOTE)
1 small white onion, sliced
mint and coriander leaves, to garnish

1 Place the chickpeas in a bowl, cover with water and leave to soak overnight. Drain, rinse and place in a large saucepan. Cover with plenty of water and bring to the boil, then reduce the heat and simmer for 40 minutes, or until soft. Drain.

2 Heat the oil in a large saucepan, add the onion and cook over medium heat for 15 minutes, or until golden brown. Add the tomato, ground coriander and cumin, chilli powder, turmeric and channa masala, and 500 ml (17 fl oz/2 cups) water and cook for 10 minutes, or until the tomato is soft. Add the chickpeas, season and cook for 7–10 minutes, or until the sauce thickens. Garnish with sliced onion and fresh mint and coriander leaves.

NOTE: *Channa (chole) masala is a spice blend available at Indian grocery stores. Garam masala can be used as a substitute but the flavour will be a little different.*

Cook the onion over medium heat for 15 minutes, or until golden brown.

Add the soaked chickpeas and cook until the sauce thickens.

NUTRITION PER SERVE
Protein 8 g; Fat 9 g; Carbohydrate 17 g; Dietary Fibre 6 g; Cholesterol 8.5 mg; 835 kJ (200 Cal)

Two-toned potato gnocchi

PREPARATION TIME: 1 HOUR 30 MINUTES | TOTAL COOKING TIME: 45 MINUTES | SERVES 6

450 g (1 lb) floury potatoes, chopped
200 g (7 oz) orange sweet potato, chopped
185 g (6½ oz/1½ cups) plain (all-purpose) flour
parmesan cheese shavings, to garnish

TOMATO AND CORIANDER SAUCE
1 tablespoon olive oil
3 garlic cloves, sliced thickly
1 onion, chopped
1 kg (2 lb 4 oz) ripe tomatoes, peeled and chopped
1 small red chilli, seeded and diced
1 large handful coriander (cilantro) leaves

NUTRITION PER SERVE
Protein 7 g; Fat 7 g; Carbohydrate 40 g; Dietary Fibre 4 g; Cholesterol 2 mg; 1060 kJ (255 Cal)

1 Steam or boil the chopped potato and sweet potato until tender and mash them in separate bowls. Add 125 g (4½ oz/1 cup) of flour with 1 teaspoon of salt to the plain potato and bring together to make a smooth dough. Add enough of the remaining flour to the sweet potato to gently bring together. The mixtures should be slightly sticky to touch. On a lightly floured surface, press the two doughs together gently until they have a two-tone appearance.

2 Divide the mixture into four and roll each, on a lightly floured surface, into a log about 2.5 cm (1 inch) thick. Slice the logs into 2 cm (¾ inch) pieces. Shape each piece into an oval and roll the gnocchi ovals onto the prongs of a floured fork. You should have about 40 pieces. Put on a lightly floured tray and cover.

3 To make the tomato and coriander sauce, heat the oil in a heavy-based saucepan, add the garlic and cook over low heat for 2 minutes, or until it just begins to brown slightly. Remove with a slotted spoon and discard. Add the onion and cook until softened. Add the tomato and bring to the boil. Reduce the heat and simmer for 30–35 minutes, stirring occasionally. Add the chilli and coriander leaves.

4 Cook the gnocchi in boiling water in batches for 2 minutes, or until they float to the surface. Remove each batch with a slotted spoon. Serve on the sauce. Garnish with parmesan.

Press the two doughs together gently until they take on a two-tone appearance.

Roll the gnocchi over the back of a fork to give the characteristic indentations.

Spinach pie

PREPARATION TIME: 25 MINUTES | TOTAL COOKING TIME: 45 MINUTES | SERVES 6

1.5 kg (3 lb 5 oz) English spinach
2 teaspoons olive oil
1 onion, chopped
4 spring onions (scallions), chopped
750 g (1 lb 10 oz/3 cups) low-fat cottage cheese
2 eggs, lightly beaten
2 garlic cloves, crushed
pinch of ground nutmeg
1 large handful mint, chopped
8 sheets filo pastry
30 g (1 oz) butter, melted
40 g (1½ oz/½ cup) fresh breadcrumbs

1 Preheat the oven to 180°C (350°F/Gas 4). Lightly spray a 1.5 litre (52 fl oz/6 cup) capacity ovenproof dish with oil. Trim and wash the spinach, then place in a large saucepan. Cover and cook for 2–3 minutes, until the spinach has just wilted. Drain, cool then squeeze dry and chop.

2 Heat the oil in a small pan. Add the onion and spring onion and cook for 2–3 minutes, until softened. Combine in a bowl with the chopped spinach. Stir in the cottage cheese, egg, garlic, nutmeg and mint. Season and mix together well.

3 Brush a sheet of filo pastry with a little butter. Fold in half widthways and line the base and sides of the dish. Repeat with three more sheets. Keep the unused sheets moist by covering with a damp tea towel (dish towel).

4 Sprinkle the breadcrumbs over the pastry. Spread the filling into the dish. Fold over any overlapping pastry. Brush and fold another sheet and place on top. Repeat with 3 more sheets. Tuck the pastry in at the sides. Brush the top with the remaining butter. Score diamonds on top using a sharp knife. Bake for 40 minutes, or until golden. Cut the pie into squares to serve.

Use your hands to squeeze the water out of the cooled spinach.

When you have covered the top with pastry, tuck it in at the sides.

NUTRITION PER SERVE

Protein 35 g; Fat 10 g; Carbohydrate 30 g; Dietary Fibre 8 g; Cholesterol 75 mg; 1500 kJ (360 Cal)

Spicy beans on baked sweet potato

PREPARATION TIME: 20 MINUTES | TOTAL COOKING TIME: 1 HOUR 30 MINUTES | SERVES 6

3 orange sweet potatoes, each about 500 g (1 lb 2 oz)
1 tablespoon olive oil
1 large onion, chopped
3 garlic cloves, crushed
2 teaspoons ground cumin
1 teaspoon ground coriander
½ teaspoon chilli powder
400 g (14 oz) tin chopped tomatoes
250 ml (9 fl oz/1 cup) vegetable stock
1 large zucchini (courgette), cubed
1 green capsicum (pepper), chopped
310 g (11 oz) tin corn kernels, drained
2 x 400 g (14 oz) tins red kidney beans, drained and rinsed
3 tablespoons chopped coriander (cilantro) leaves
light sour cream and grated low-fat cheddar cheese, to serve

1 Preheat the oven to 210°C (415°F/Gas 6–7). Rinse the sweet potatoes, then pierce with a sharp knife. Place them on a baking tray and bake for 1–1½ hours, or until soft. Meanwhile, heat the oil in a saucepan and cook the onion over medium heat for 5 minutes, stirring occasionally, until soft. Add the garlic and spices, and cook, stirring, for 1 minute.

2 Add the tomato and stock, stir well, then add the vegetables and beans. Bring to the boil, then reduce the heat and simmer, partially covered, for 20 minutes. Uncover, increase the heat slightly, and cook for a further 10–15 minutes, or until the liquid has reduced and thickened. Stir in the coriander leaves just before serving.

3 To serve, cut the sweet potatoes in half lengthways. Spoon the vegetable mixture over the top. Add a dollop of sour cream and sprinkle with grated cheddar cheese.

NUTRITION PER SERVE
Protein 15 g; Fat 5 g; Carbohydrate 72 g; Dietary Fibre 17 g; Cholesterol 0 mg; 1665 kJ (397 Cal)

Cook the spicy vegetable mixture until the liquid has reduced.

Cut the baked sweet potatoes in half lengthways and top with the spicy vegetables.

Asian mushroom risotto

PREPARATION TIME: 20 MINUTES + 20 MINUTES SOAKING | TOTAL COOKING TIME: 45 MINUTES | SERVES 4

10 g (¼ oz) dried Chinese mushrooms
500 ml (17 fl oz/2 cups) vegetable stock
2 tablespoons soy sauce
4 tablespoons mirin
150 g (5½ oz) Swiss brown mushrooms
150 g (5½ oz) oyster mushrooms
100 g (3½ oz) fresh shiitake mushrooms
150 g (5½ oz) shimeji mushrooms
1 tablespoon butter
1 tablespoon olive oil
1 onion, finely chopped
3 garlic cloves, crushed
1 tablespoon finely chopped fresh ginger
440 g (15½ oz/2 cups) arborio rice
100 g (3½ oz) enoki mushrooms, trimmed
2 tablespoons snipped fresh chives
shaved parmesan cheese, to garnish

NUTRITION PER SERVE
Protein 17 g; Fat 15 g; Carbohydrate 92 g; Dietary Fibre 8 g; Cholesterol 28 mg; 2397 kJ (573 Cal)

1 Put the Chinese mushrooms in a bowl, cover with 625 ml (21½ fl oz/2½ cups) hot water and soak for 20 minutes, then drain, reserving the liquid. Remove the stems and thinly slice the caps.

2 Heat the vegetable stock, soy sauce, mirin, reserved mushroom liquid and 250 ml (9 fl oz/1 cup) water in a large saucepan. Bring to the boil, then keep at a low simmer, skimming off any scum that forms on the surface.

3 Trim and slice the Swiss brown, oyster and shiitake mushrooms, discarding any woody ends. Trim the shimeji and pull apart into small clumps. Melt the butter in a large saucepan over medium heat, add all the mushrooms except the Chinese and enoki and cook, stirring, for 3 minutes, or until wilted, then remove from the pan.

4 Add the oil to the pan, then add the chopped onion and cook, stirring, for 4–5 minutes, or until soft and just starting to brown. Add the garlic and ginger and stir well until fragrant. Add the rice and stir for 1 minute, or until it is well coated in the oil mixture.

5 Gradually add 125 ml (4 fl oz/½ cup) of the hot stock to the rice. Stir over medium heat until nearly all the liquid has been absorbed. Continue adding more stock, a little at a time stirring for 20–25 minutes, until all the stock has been absorbed and the rice is tender. Add all the mushrooms and stir well. Season and garnish with the chives and shaved parmesan.

Divide the shimeji and slice the Swiss brown, oyster and shiitake mushrooms.

Stir the rice constantly until nearly all the liquid has been absorbed.

Pasta primavera

PREPARATION TIME: 35 MINUTES | TOTAL COOKING TIME: 15 MINUTES | SERVES 6

500 g (1 lb 2 oz) pasta
150 g (5½ oz) fresh asparagus spears
150 g (5½ oz/1 cup) frozen (or fresh) broad (fava) beans
30 g (1 oz) butter
1 celery stalk, sliced
155 g (5½ oz/1 cup) peas
250 ml (9 fl oz/1 cup) light pouring (whipping) cream
50 g (1¾ oz/½ cup) grated parmesan cheese

1 Cook the pasta in a large saucepan of rapidly boiling salted water until *al dente*. Drain and return to the pan.

2 Meanwhile, snap the woody ends from the asparagus and cut into small pieces. Bring a saucepan of water to the boil, add the asparagus and cook for 2 minutes. Using a slotted spoon, remove the asparagus from the pan and plunge the pieces into a bowl of ice-cold water to stop the cooking process.

3 Add the broad beans to the saucepan of boiling water. Remove immediately and cool in cold water. Drain, then peel by squeezing the beans out of their skins. If fresh broad beans are used, cook them for 2–5 minutes or until tender. If the beans are young, the skin can be left on, but old beans should be peeled.

4 Heat the butter in a heavy-based frying pan. Add the celery and stir for 2 minutes. Add the peas and the cream and cook gently for 3 minutes. Add the asparagus, broad beans, parmesan, and salt and pepper. Bring the sauce to the boil and cook for 1 minute. Add the sauce to the cooked pasta and toss well to combine.

NOTE: *Spring vegetables are generally used for primavera. Choose your favourite from leeks, zucchini, beans or sugarsnap peas.*

NUTRITION PER SERVE
Protein 20 g; Fat 10 g; Carbohydrate 95 g; Dietary Fibre 10 g; Cholesterol 5 mg; 2295 kJ (545 Cal)

Bend the asparagus spear gently and the woody end will snap off.

After cooking, squeeze the broad beans from their skins. If they are stubborn, slit with a knife.

Asian barley pilau

PREPARATION TIME: 10 MINUTES + 15 MINUTES STANDING | TOTAL COOKING TIME: 35 MINUTES | SERVES 4

15 g (½ oz) dried sliced mushrooms
500 ml (17 fl oz/2 cups) vegetable stock
125 ml (4 fl oz/½ cup) dry sherry
1 tablespoon oil
3 large French shallots (eschalots), thinly sliced
2 large garlic cloves, crushed
1 tablespoon grated fresh ginger
1 teaspoon sichuan peppercorns, crushed (see NOTE)
330 g (11½ oz/1½ cups) pearl barley
500 g (1 lb 2 oz) choy sum, cut into short lengths
3 teaspoons kecap manis (see NOTE, page 13)
1 teaspoon sesame oil

1 Place the mushrooms in a bowl and cover with boiling water, then leave for 15 minutes. Strain, reserving 125 ml (4 fl oz/½ cup) of the soaking liquid.

2 Bring the stock and sherry to the boil in a saucepan, then reduce the heat, cover and simmer until needed.

3 Heat the oil in a large saucepan and cook the shallots over medium heat for 2–3 minutes, or until soft. Add the garlic, ginger and peppercorns and cook for 1 minute. Add the barley and mushrooms and mix well. Stir in the stock and mushroom liquid, then reduce the heat and simmer, covered, for 25 minutes, or until the liquid has evaporated.

4 Meanwhile, steam the choy sum until wilted. Add to the barley mixture. Stir in the kecap manis and sesame oil to serve.

NOTE: *You can buy sichuan peppercorns at Asian food stores.*

NUTRITION PER SERVE
Protein 13 g; Fat 8.5 g; Carbohydrate 52 g; Dietary Fibre 13 g; Cholesterol 0 mg; 1552 kJ (370 Cal)

Use a mortar and pestle to crush the sichuan peppercorns. This will release their flavour.

Strain the mushrooms, reserving some of the liquid for flavouring the pilau.

Vegetable strudel parcels

PREPARATION TIME: 1 HOUR | TOTAL COOKING TIME: 30 MINUTES | SERVES 4

300 g (10½ oz) pumpkin (winter squash)
2 carrots
1 parsnip
2 celery stalks
2 teaspoons sesame oil
1 onion, finely sliced
3 teaspoons finely chopped or grated fresh ginger
1 tablespoon dry sherry
1 teaspoon finely grated lemon zest
185 g (6½ oz/1 cup) cooked long-grain rice
2 tablespoons plum sauce
1 tablespoon sweet chilli sauce
2 teaspoons soy sauce
16 sheets filo pastry
35 g (1¼ oz/⅓ cup) dry breadcrumbs
1 teaspoon butter, melted
1 tablespoon sesame seeds
sweet chilli sauce, for serving

NUTRITION PER SERVE
Protein 15 g; Fat 8 g; Carbohydrate 95 g; Dietary Fibre 7 g; Cholesterol 3 mg; 2210 kJ (530 Cal)

1 Cut the pumpkin, carrots, parsnip and celery into thick matchsticks about 3 mm (⅛ inch) wide and 5 cm (2 inches) long. Heat the oil in a wok, add the onion and ginger and stir-fry, tossing well until brown, over medium heat. Add the pumpkin, carrot and parsnip, toss well and cook for 1 minute. Sprinkle 2 teaspoons water over the vegetables, cover and steam for 1 minute. Add the celery, sherry and zest, toss and cook for 1 minute. Cover and let steam for 1 minute, or until tender. Stir in the cooked rice and the plum, chilli and soy sauces. Set aside for about 20 minutes to cool.

2 Preheat the oven to 190°C (375°F/Gas 5). Remove two sheets of pastry, keeping the remaining pastry covered with a damp tea towel (dish towel). Place one sheet on top of the other, brush the edges with a little water, then scatter some breadcrumbs over the pastry. Top with another two sheets of pastry, fold over the edges to make a 2 cm (¾ inch) border and brush with a little water. Press the edges down with your fingertips.

3 Place one-quarter of the filling about 5 cm (2 inches) from the short end, then firmly roll into a parcel to encase the filling, ensuring that the seam is underneath. Repeat with the remaining ingredients. Brush the tops very lightly with butter, cut three slashes across the top of each parcel and scatter any remaining breadcrumbs and the sesame seeds over the top. Arrange on a lightly greased baking tray and bake for 20–25 minutes, or until crisp and golden. Serve immediately, drizzled with sweet chilli sauce.

Moisten the pastry before scattering the breadcrumbs over it.

Fold the pastry edges over, brush with water, then press down lightly.

Put the filling on the pastry, then firmly roll it up into a parcel.

GMP

Layered country cob

PREPARATION TIME: 40 MINUTES + OVERNIGHT REFRIGERATION | TOTAL COOKING TIME: 25 MINUTES | SERVES 8

2 red capsicums (peppers)
1 eggplant (aubergine), thinly sliced
1 large red onion, thinly sliced
450 g (1 lb) white cob loaf
1 tablespoon olive oil
2 garlic cloves, finely chopped
1 teaspoon chopped lemon thyme
250 g (9 oz) English spinach
350 g (12 oz) ricotta cheese

1 Preheat the grill (broiler) to hot. Cut the capsicum in quarters lengthways and remove the seeds and membrane. Arrange the capsicum, skin side up, and the eggplant, sprayed lightly with oil, on the grill. Grill (broil) for about 7 minutes, turning the eggplant over as it browns and until the capsicum skin is blackened and blistered, then leave to cool. Grill the onion for about 6 minutes, turning once, until softened. Peel the skin away from the capsicum.

2 Cut the top off the cob and pull out the centre. Combine the oil, garlic and thyme and brush lightly inside the shell. Put the spinach leaves in a bowl and pour boiling water over to cover. Allow to soften for 1 minute, rinse with cold water until cool, then drain and pat dry with paper towels.

3 To fill the cob, arrange half the eggplant in the base, followed by capsicum and onion, then a layer of ricotta, spinach and the remaining eggplant. Season between layers. Press down firmly. If the top of the cob is empty, fill the space with a little of the soft bread from the centre. Replace the top of the loaf and wrap the whole thing securely with foil. Top with a brick wrapped in foil, or a heavy bowl to weigh it down. Refrigerate overnight. Cut into wedges to serve.

Cut the top off the cob loaf and pull the bread from the centre.

Put half the eggplant in the cob, then capsicum and onion.

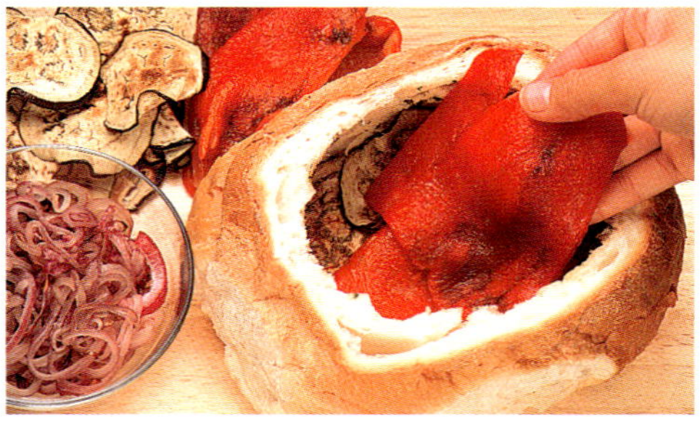

NUTRITION PER SERVE
Protein 10 g; Fat 9 g; Carbohydrate 30 g; Dietary Fibre 4 g; Cholesterol 20 mg; 1040 kJ (250 Cal)

Pasta pomodoro

PREPARATION TIME: 15 MINUTES | TOTAL COOKING TIME: 15 MINUTES | SERVES 4

500 g (1 lb 2 oz) pasta
1 tablespoon olive oil
1 onion, finely chopped
2 x 400 g (14 oz) tins chopped tomatoes
1 small handful basil leaves

1 Cook the pasta in a large saucepan of rapidly boiling salted water until *al dente*. Drain, return to the pan and keep warm.

2 Heat the oil in a large frying pan. Add the onion and cook over medium heat until softened. Stir in the tomato and simmer for 5–6 minutes, or until the sauce has reduced slightly and thickened. Season with salt and pepper. Stir in the basil leaves and cook for another minute.

3 Pour the sauce over the warm pasta and gently toss through. Serve immediately.

NUTRITION PER SERVE
Protein 20 g; Fat 10 g; Carbohydrate 95 g; Dietary Fibre 10 g; Cholesterol 0 mg; 2295 kJ (545 Cal)

To finely chop the onion, use a very sharp knife and make cuts close together.

Desserts and sweet things

Almond and pear crêpes

PREPARATION TIME: 45 MINUTES + 10 MINUTES STANDING | TOTAL COOKING TIME: 40 MINUTES | MAKES 4

4 beurre bosc (or any firm) pears
3 tablespoons dry white wine
60 g (2¼ oz/¼ cup) caster (superfine) sugar
1 cinnamon stick
2 cloves
1 vanilla bean
4 dates, roughly chopped
2 tablespoons sultanas (golden raisins)
85 g (3 oz/⅔ cup) plain (all-purpose) flour
1 egg, lightly beaten
250 ml (9 fl oz/1 cup) skim milk
cooking oil spray
2 tablespoons ground almonds
1 tablespoon soft brown sugar
½ teaspoon ground cinnamon
2 teaspoons flaked almonds
icing (confectioners') sugar, for dusting

STRAWBERRY SAUCE

125 g (4½ oz) strawberries, chopped
1 teaspoon caster (superfine) sugar
2 tablespoons orange juice

NUTRITION PER SERVE
Protein 9.5 g; Fat 7 g; Carbohydrate 80 g; Dietary Fibre 7 g; Cholesterol 45 mg; 1740 kJ (415 Cal)

1 Remove the cores of the pears using a melon baller, then peel. Combine 500 ml (17 fl oz/2 cups) water with the wine, sugar, cinnamon stick and cloves in a saucepan large enough to fit the pears. Split the bean in half lengthways and scrape the seeds out. Add the seeds to the pan with the bean and stir over medium heat until the sugar has dissolved. Add the pears and simmer, covered, for about 20 minutes. Remove from the heat and allow to cool in the syrup. Drain and stand the pears on paper towels. Fill the base of each with the dates and sultanas.

2 To make the crepes, sift the flour into a bowl, gradually beat in the egg and milk, beating until smooth. Strain into a bowl and set aside for 10 minutes. Preheat the oven to 200°C (400°F/Gas 6). Lightly oil a 24 cm (9½ inch) non-stick frying pan with oil spray, heat the pan and pour in a quarter of the batter, swirling to cover the base of the pan. Cook until lightly browned, turn and brown the other side. Remove and repeat with the remaining mixture.

3 Place the crepes on a work surface, place a quarter of the ground almonds, brown sugar and cinnamon in the centre of each and top with a pear. Gather the crepes around the pears and tie with string. Sprinkle with the flaked almonds. Bake on a lightly oiled baking tray for about 5 minutes. Discard the string.

4 To make the strawberry sauce, blend all the ingredients in a blender until smooth and then strain. Dust the pear crepes with icing sugar and serve with strawberry sauce.

Use a melon baller to remove the cores from the pears through the bases.

Combine the dates and sultanas and fill the base of each pear.

Gather the crepes around the pears and tie together with string.

Passionfruit bavarois

PREPARATION TIME: 10 MINUTES + OVERNIGHT REFRIGERATION | TOTAL COOKING TIME: NIL | SERVES 8

2 x 170 g (5¾ oz) tins passionfruit in syrup
300 g (10½ oz) silken tofu, chopped
600 ml (21 fl oz) buttermilk
2 tablespoons caster (superfine) sugar
1 teaspoon vanilla essence
2½ tablespoons gelatine
185 ml (6 fl oz/¾ cup) passionfruit pulp

1 Push the passionfruit in syrup through a sieve. Discard the seeds. Combine the strained syrup with the tofu, buttermilk, caster sugar and vanilla in a blender. Blend for 90 seconds on high, to mix thoroughly. Leave in the blender.

2 Put 4 tablespoons water in a small bowl and put the bowl in a slightly larger bowl of boiling water. Sprinkle the gelatine onto the water in the small bowl and stir until dissolved. Leave to cool.

3 Place eight 200 ml (7 fl oz) dariole moulds in a baking dish. Add the gelatine to the blender and mix on high for 1 minute. Pour into the moulds, cover the dish with plastic wrap and refrigerate overnight.

4 When ready to serve, carefully run a spatula around the edge of each mould and dip the bases into hot water for 2 seconds to make removal easier. Place each on a plate and spoon the passionfruit pulp over the top and around the bases.

Blend the strained passionfruit syrup, tofu, buttermilk, sugar and vanilla.

Sprinkle the gelatine over the surface of the water in a small bowl.

NUTRITION PER SERVE
Protein 8 g; Fat 2.5 g; Carbohydrate 10 g; Dietary Fibre 10 g; Cholesterol 3 mg; 455 kJ (110 Cal)

Watermelon and vodka granita

PREPARATION TIME: 10 MINUTES + 5 HOURS FREEZING | TOTAL COOKING TIME: NIL | SERVES 6

1 kg (2 lb 4 oz) piece of watermelon, rind removed (to leave 600 g/1 lb 5 oz)
2 teaspoons lime juice
60 g (2 oz/¼ cup) caster (superfine) sugar
3 tablespoons citrus-flavoured vodka

1 Coarsely chop the watermelon, removing the seeds. Place the flesh in a food processor and add the lime juice and sugar. Process until smooth, then strain through a fine sieve. Stir in the vodka, then taste—if the watermelon is not very sweet, you may have to add a little more sugar.

2 Pour into a shallow 1.5 litre (52 fl oz/6 cup) metal tin and freeze for about 1 hour, or until beginning to freeze around the edges. Scrape the frozen parts back into the mixture with a fork. Repeat every 30 minutes for another 4 hours, or until even ice crystals have formed.

3 Beat with a fork just before serving. To serve, scrape into dishes with a fork.

SERVING SUGGESTION: *A scoop of the granita in a shot glass with vodka is great for summer cocktail parties.*

NUTRITION PER SERVE
Protein 0.5 g; Fat 0 g; Carbohydrate 18 g; Dietary Fibre 1 g; Cholesterol 0 mg; 410 kJ (98 Cal)

Coarsely chop the watermelon flesh, removing the seeds.

Scrape the frozen parts around the edge back into the mixture.

Scrape the frozen par s every 30 minutes until even ice crystals form.

Figs with orange cream and raisins

PREPARATION TIME: 20 MINUTES + 1 HOUR SOAKING | TOTAL COOKING TIME: 12 MINUTES | SERVES 4

150 g (5½ oz/1¼ cups) raisins
4 tablespoons tawny port
1 tablespoon custard powder
250 ml (9 fl oz/1 cup) skim milk
1 tablespoon sugar
100 g (3½ oz) ricotta cheese
200 g (7 oz) low-fat fromage frais or light vanilla Fruche
zest strips and juice of 1 orange
1 teaspoon ground cinnamon
8 fresh figs

NUTRITION PER SERVE
Protein 7 g; Fat 3.5 g; Carbohydrate 45 g; Dietary Fibre 4.5 g; Cholesterol 15 mg; 1510 kJ (360 Cal)

1 Soak the raisins in the tawny port for 1 hour, or until plumped up.

2 In a small saucepan, blend the custard powder with the skim milk, add the sugar and stir over low heat until dissolved. Increase the heat and stir until the custard boils and thickens. Remove from the heat immediately, pour into a small bowl and cover with plastic wrap. Cool completely. Transfer to an electric mixer, add the ricotta and fromage frais and beat until smooth.

3 Warm the raisin mixture with the orange zest, juice and cinnamon in a small saucepan. Cover and keep warm.

4 Starting from the top, cut the figs into quarters, slicing only two-thirds of the way down so they hold together. Transfer to ramekins or a serving dish or platter. Place 2 heaped tablespoons of the custard cream mixture into the centre of each fig, top with a spoonful of the warm raisin and orange mixture and serve at once.

Stir the custard continuously until it boils and thickens, then remove from the heat.

When the custard has cooled, mix it with the ricotta and fromage frais.

Cut the figs into quarters, slicing only two-thirds of the way down.

Creamy rice pots

PREPARATION TIME: 15 MINUTES | TOTAL COOKING TIME: 1 HOUR | SERVES 4

110 g (3¾ oz/½ cup) short-grain rice
1 litre (35 fl oz/4 cups) skim milk
60 g (2¼ oz/¼ cup) caster (superfine) sugar
1 teaspoon grated orange zest
1 teaspoon grated lemon zest
1 teaspoon vanilla essence
20 g (¾ oz) hazelnuts
1 tablespoon soft brown sugar

1 Wash the rice in a sieve, then drain thoroughly. Combine the skim milk and caster sugar in a non-stick saucepan and stir over low heat until dissolved. Add the rice and zest and stir briefly. Bring to the boil and reduce the heat to as low as possible. Cook for 1 hour, stirring occasionally, until the rice is tender and the mixture thick and creamy. Stir in the vanilla essence.

2 While the rice is cooking, spread the hazelnuts on a baking tray and toast in a moderate 180°C (350°F/Gas 4) oven for about 5 minutes. Rub the hot nuts in a tea towel (dish towel) to remove as much of the skin as possible. Cool and then grind in a food processor until coarsely chopped.

3 Spoon the rice into four heatproof 185 ml (6 fl oz/¾ cup) capacity ramekins. Combine the brown sugar and ground hazelnuts and sprinkle over the surface of the rice. Cook briefly under a very hot grill (broiler) until the sugar melts and the nuts are lightly browned. Serve immediately.

Cook the rice mixture over very low heat until thick and creamy.

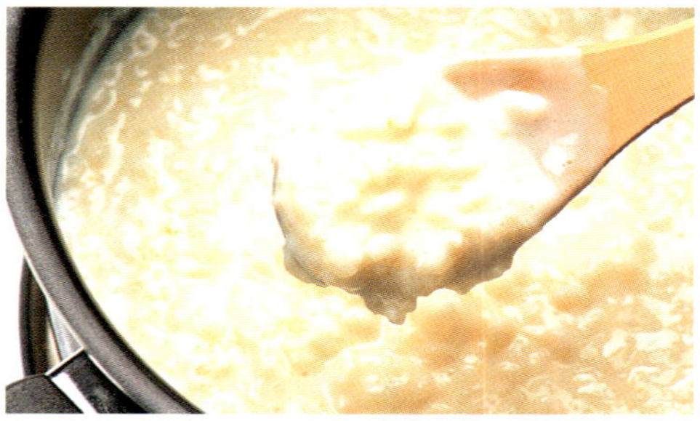

Transfer the hot nuts to a tea towel and rub to remove as much skin as possible.

NUTRITION PER SERVE
Protein 12 g; Fat 3.5 g; Carbohydrate 55 g; Dietary Fibre 1 g; Cholesterol 7 mg; 1235 kJ (295 Cal)

Brazil nut and coffee biscotti

PREPARATION TIME: 20 MINUTES | TOTAL COOKING TIME: 45 MINUTES | MAKES 40 PIECES

3 teaspoons instant coffee powder
1 tablespoon dark rum, warmed
2 eggs
125 g (4½ oz/½ cup) caster (superfine) sugar
155 g (5½ oz/1¼ cups) plain (all-purpose) flour
60 g (2¼ oz/½ cup) self-raising flour
1 teaspoon ground cinnamon
105 g (3½ oz/¾ cup) Brazil nuts, roughly chopped
1 tablespoon caster (superfine) sugar, extra

1 Preheat the oven to 180°C (350°F/Gas 4). Dissolve the coffee in the rum. Beat the eggs and sugar until thick and creamy, then beat in the coffee. Sift the flours and cinnamon into a bowl, then stir in the nuts. Mix in the egg mixture.

2 Divide the mixture into two rolls, each about 28 cm (11¼ inches) long. Line a baking tray with baking paper, put the rolls on it and press lightly to flatten to about 6 cm (2½ inches) across. Brush lightly with water and sprinkle with the extra sugar. Bake for 25 minutes, or until firm and light brown. Cool until warm on the tray. Reduce the oven temperature to 160°C (315°F/Gas 2–3).

3 Cut into 1 cm (½ inch) thick diagonal slices. Bake in a single layer on the lined tray for 20 minutes, or until dry, turning once. Cool on a rack. When cold, these can be stored in an airtight container for 2–3 weeks.

Beat the coffee and rum mixture into the beaten eggs and sugar.

Put the rolls of dough on the lined baking tray and press lightly into shape.

NUTRITION PER BISCOTTI
Protein 1 g; Fat 1.5 g; Carbohydrate 7.5 g; Dietary Fibre 0 g; Cholesterol 9 mg; 210 kJ (50 Cal)

Tiramisu

PREPARATION TIME: 15 MINUTES + OVERNIGHT REFRIGERATION | TOTAL COOKING TIME: 5 MINUTES | SERVES 6

3 tablespoons custard powder
250 ml (9 fl oz/1 cup) skim milk
2 tablespoons caster (superfine) sugar
2 teaspoons vanilla essence
2 x 130 g (4½ oz) tubs low-fat fromage frais or light vanilla Fruche
2 egg whites
420 ml (14½ fl oz/1⅔ cups) prepared strong coffee, cooled
2 tablespoons amaretto
250 g (9 oz) savoiardi (lady fingers) biscuits
2 tablespoons unsweetened dark cocoa powder

NUTRITION PER SERVE
Protein 5 g; Fat 5.5 g; Carbohydrate 26 g; Dietary Fibre 1 g; Cholesterol 7.5 mg; 754 kJ (180 Cal)

1 Stir the custard powder in a small saucepan with 2 tablespoons of the milk until dissolved. Add the remaining milk, sugar and vanilla and stir over medium heat until the mixture boils and thickens. Remove from the heat. This custard will be thicker than the usual custard. Transfer to a bowl, cover the surface with plastic wrap and cool at room temperature.

2 Using electric beaters, mix the custard and the fromage frais in a bowl. Beat for 2 minutes. In a small bowl, whip the egg whites until soft peaks form, then fold into the custard mixture.

3 Pour the coffee into a dish and add the amaretto. Quickly dip the biscuits, one at a time, in the coffee mixture, just enough to cover (dip quickly, or they'll be soggy) and arrange in a single layer over the base of a 2.75 litre (96 fl oz/11 cup) dish.

4 Using half the cream mixture, smooth it evenly over the biscuits. Dust half the dark cocoa over the cream and then repeat the layers with the remaining biscuits and cream. Cover with plastic wrap. Refrigerate overnight, or for at least 6 hours. Dust with dark cocoa powder to serve.

Stir the custard powder in a small amount of milk until dissolved.

Fold the whipped egg whites into the custard mixture with a large metal spoon.

Dip the biscuits quickly into the coffee mixture to cover evenly.

Poached pears in saffron citrus syrup

PREPARATION TIME: 10 MINUTES | TOTAL COOKING TIME: 30 MINUTES | SERVES 4

1 vanilla bean, split lengthways
½ teaspoon firmly packed saffron threads
185 g (6½ oz/heaped ¾ cup) caster (superfine) sugar
2 teaspoons grated lemon zest
4 pears, peeled
biscotti, to serve (see NOTE)

1 Place the vanilla bean, saffron threads, sugar, lemon zest and 500 ml (17 fl oz/2 cups) water in a large saucepan and mix together well. Heat, stirring, over low heat until the sugar has dissolved. Bring to the boil, then reduce to a gentle simmer.

2 Add the pears and cook, covered, for 12–15 minutes, or until tender when tested with a metal skewer. Turn the pears over with a slotted spoon halfway through cooking. Once cooked, remove from the syrup with a slotted spoon.

3 Leave uncovered and allow the saffron citrus syrup to come to the boil. Cook for 8–10 minutes, or until the syrup has reduced by half and thickened slightly. Remove the vanilla bean and drizzle the syrup over the pears. Serve with biscotti.

NOTE: *Biscotti are available in a wide variety of flavours. You can buy biscotti at gourmet food stores, delicatessens and supermarkets or use the* *recipe on page 217.*

Stir the saffron citrus syrup until the sugar has completely dissolved.

Cook the pears until tender when tested with a metal skewer.

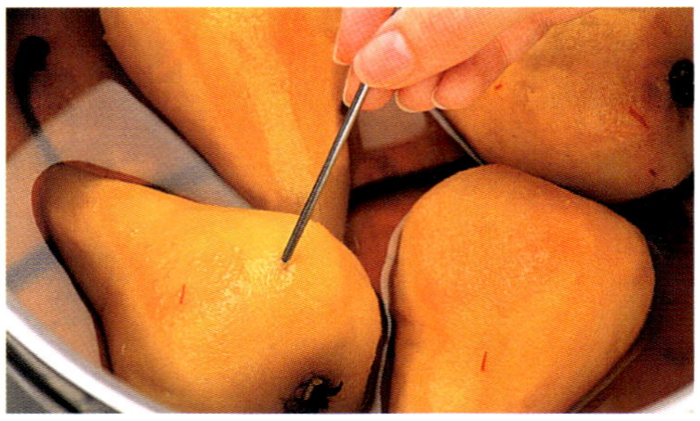

NUTRITION PER SERVE
Protein 0.5 g; Fat 0 g; Carbohydrate 70 g; Dietary Fibre 4.5 g; Cholesterol 0 mg; 1155 kJ (276 Cal)

Berries in Champagne jelly

PREPARATION TIME: 10 MINUTES + REFRIGERATION | TOTAL COOKING TIME: 5 MINUTES | SERVES 8

1 litre (35 fl oz/4 cups) Champagne or sparkling white wine
1½ tablespoons gelatine
250 g (9 oz/1 cup) sugar
4 strips lemon zest
4 strips orange zest
250 g (9 oz/1⅔ cups) small strawberries, hulled
250 g (9 oz/1⅔ cups) blueberries

1 Pour 500 ml (17 fl oz/2 cups) Champagne or sparkling white wine into a bowl and let the bubbles subside. Sprinkle the gelatine over the top in an even layer. Leave until the gelatine is spongy—do not stir. Place the remaining Champagne in a large saucepan with the sugar, lemon and orange zest and heat gently, stirring, until all the sugar has dissolved.

2 Remove the pan from the heat, add the gelatine mixture and stir until thoroughly dissolved. Leave the jelly to cool completely, then remove the lemon and orange zest.

3 Divide the strawberries and blueberries among eight 125 ml (4 fl oz/½ cup) glasses or bowls and pour the jelly over them. Chill until the jelly has fully set. Remove from the fridge 15 minutes before serving.

Sprinkle the gelatine over the Champagne in an even layer and leave until spongy.

Pour the jelly into the wine glasses or bowls, covering the berries

NUTRITION PER SERVE
Protein 3 g; Fat 0 g; Carbohydrate 37 g; Dietary Fibre 1.5 g; Cholesterol 0 mg; 965 kJ (230 Cal)

Chestnut hearts

PREPARATION TIME: 40 MINUTES | TOTAL COOKING TIME: 40 MINUTES | MAKES 30 HEARTS

150 g (5½ oz/⅔ cup) caster (superfine) sugar
2 eggs
2½ teaspoons coconut essence
6 egg whites
1 teaspoon cream of tartar
155 g (5½ oz/1¼ cups) self-raising flour, sifted
250 g (9 oz/1 cup) tinned sweetened chestnut purée
90 g (3¼ oz/⅓ cup) ricotta cheese
2 teaspoons cocoa powder
icing (confectioners') sugar, to dust

NUTRITION PER HEART
Protein 1 g; Fat 1 g; Carbohydrate 8 g; Dietary Fibre 0.5 g; Cholesterol 8.5 mg; 175 kJ (40 Cal)

1 Preheat the oven to 180°C (350°F/Gas 4). Lightly spray two 20 x 30 cm (8 x 12 inch) shallow baking tins with oil and line with baking paper.

2 Beat the sugar and eggs in a bowl with electric beaters for 3–4 minutes, until light and fluffy. Transfer to a large bowl. Add the coconut essence.

3 Beat the egg whites until foamy. Add the cream of tartar and beat until firm peaks form. Stir a third of the egg white into the creamed mixture. Slowly fold in the flour in small batches, alternating with small amounts of egg white. Fold in both until just combined. Divide the mixture between the trays. Bake for 20–25 minutes, until golden. Test with a skewer. Turn out onto cooling racks lined with baking paper. Leave until completely cold (if possible, make a day in advance).

4 In a blender, mix the chestnut purée with the ricotta and cocoa until very smooth. Slice the cakes in half horizontally and join with the chestnut mixture. Cut out heart shapes using a 5 cm (2 inch) heart-shaped cookie cutter. Clean the cutter between cuts or dust it in icing sugar if the cake sticks. Dust with icing sugar before serving.

Beat the sugar and eggs together until the mixture is light and fluffy.

Once the cakes are completely cooled, slice in half horizontally.

When the cakes are joined with the chestnut mixture, cut out heart shapes.

Banana pancakes

PREPARATION TIME: 20 MINUTES + 1 HOUR | TOTAL COOKING TIME: 25 MINUTES | MAKES 10

2 very ripe bananas, mashed
150 g (5½ oz/1 cup) wholemeal (whole-wheat) flour
2 teaspoons baking powder
½ teaspoon ground cinnamon
pinch ground nutmeg
250 ml (9 fl oz/1 cup) skim milk
1 tablespoon maple syrup
cooking oil spray
maple syrup and banana, for serving

1 Put the mashed banana in a large bowl. Sift the flour, baking powder, cinnamon and nutmeg onto the banana and return the husks to the bowl. Stir until the flour is moistened but not totally combined with the mashed banana.

2 Make a well in the centre, add the milk and syrup and stir constantly until smooth. Set aside for 1 hour.

3 Heat a large non-stick frying pan over medium heat and coat with oil spray. Cook the pancakes in batches, using 3 tablespoons of batter for each pancake. Cook for 3–4 minutes, or until small bubbles appear on the surface. Using a spatula, gently turn the pancakes over, loosening the edges first so they don't stick to the pan. Cook for another 3 minutes. Remove from the pan and keep warm. Spray the pan with a little oil after each batch and continue with the remaining mixture. Serve drizzled with maple syrup and a few slices of banana.

When you have sifted the wholemeal flour, return the husks to the bowl.

Cook the pancakes over medium heat until small bubbles appear on the surface.

NUTRITION PER PANCAKE
Protein 3 g; Fat 0.5 g; Carbohydrate 17 g; Dietary Fibre 2 g; Cholesterol 1 mg; 350 kJ (85 Cal)

Mango and passionfruit sorbet

PREPARATION TIME: 20 MINUTES + 8 HOURS FREEZING | TOTAL COOKING TIME: 5 MINUTES | SERVES 6

250 g (9 oz/1 cup) caster (superfine) sugar
90 g (3¼ oz/⅓ cup) passionfruit pulp
½ large mango, about 200 g (7 oz), chopped
1 large peach, about 250 g (9 oz), chopped
2 tablespoons lemon juice
1 egg white

1 Stir the sugar in a saucepan with 250 ml (9 fl oz/1 cup) water over low heat until dissolved. Increase the heat, bring to the boil and boil for 1 minute. Transfer to a glass bowl, cool, then refrigerate. Strain the passionfruit pulp, reserving 1 tablespoon of the seeds.

2 Blend the fruit, passionfruit juice and lemon juice in a blender until smooth. With the motor running, add the cold sugar syrup and 150 ml (5 fl oz) water. Stir in the passionfruit seeds. Freeze in a shallow container, stirring occasionally, for about 5 hours, or until almost set.

3 Break up the icy mixture roughly with a fork or spoon, transfer to a bowl and beat with electric beaters until smooth and fluffy. Beat the egg white in a small bowl until firm peaks form, then fold into the mixture until just combined. Spread into a loaf tin and return to the freezer until firm. Transfer to the refrigerator, to soften, 15 minutes before serving.

VARIATION: *To make a berry sorbet, use 200 g (7 oz) blackberries or blueberries, 200 g (7 oz) hulled strawberries and 50 g (1¾ oz) peach flesh. Prepare as above.*

Leave the motor running and pour in the cold sugar syrup and water.

Gently fold the egg white into the smooth fruit purée with a metal spoon.

NUTRITION PER SERVE
Protein 2 g; Fat 0 g; Carbohydrate 50 g; Dietary Fibre 3 g; Cholesterol 0 mg; 850 kJ (200 Cal)

Lemon berry cheesecake

PREPARATION TIME: 25 MINUTES + OVERNIGHT REFRIGERATION | TOTAL COOKING TIME: NIL | SERVES 12

60 g (2¼ oz) plain biscuits (cookies), finely crushed
30 g (1 oz) butter, melted
300 g (10½ oz) ricotta cheese
2 tablespoons caster (superfine) sugar
2 x 130 g (4¼ oz) tubs low-fat fromage frais or light vanilla Fruche
2 x 130 g (4½ oz) tubs low-fat lemon fromage frais or light lemon Fruche
2 teaspoons finely grated lemon zest
2 tablespoons fresh lemon juice
1 tablespoon gelatine
2 egg whites
250 g (9 oz) strawberries, halved

1 Lightly oil and line the base and sides of a 20 cm (8 inch) diameter spring-form cake tin with plastic wrap. Combine the biscuit crumbs and butter in a small bowl and press evenly over the base of the tin. Refrigerate while making the filling.

2 Combine the ricotta and sugar in a food processor until smooth. Add all the fromage frais, the lemon zest and juice and mix well. Put 3 tablespoons water in a small bowl, sprinkle the gelatine in an even layer onto the surface and leave to go spongy. Bring a small saucepan of water to the boil, remove from the heat and put the gelatine bowl in the pan. The water should come halfway up the side of the bowl. Stir the gelatine until clear and dissolved, then cool slightly. Stir the gelatine mixture into the ricotta mixture, then transfer to a large bowl. Beat the egg whites until soft peaks form, then fold into the ricotta mixture.

3 Pour the mixture into the prepared tin and refrigerate for several hours or overnight, until set. Carefully remove from the tin by removing the side and gently easing the plastic from underneath. Decorate with the halved strawberries.

NUTRITION PER SERVE
Protein 5 g; Fat 6 g; Carbohydrate 8 g; Dietary Fibre 1 g; Cholesterol 15 mg; 425 kJ (100 Cal)

Combine the biscuit crumbs and butter, then press evenly over the base of the tin.

Gently fold the beaten egg white into the ricotta mixture with a large metal spoon.

Fudge brownies

PREPARATION TIME: 15 MINUTES | TOTAL COOKING TIME: 30 MINUTES | MAKES 18 PIECES

cooking oil spray
60 g (2¼ oz/½ cup) plain (all-purpose) flour
60 g (2¼ oz/½ cup) self-raising flour
1 teaspoon bicarbonate of soda (baking soda)
90 g (3¼ oz/¾ cup) cocoa powder
2 eggs
310 g (11 oz/1⅓ cups) caster (superfine) sugar
2 teaspoons vanilla essence
2 tablespoons vegetable oil
200 g (7 oz) low-fat fromage frais
140 g (5 oz) apple purée
icing (confectioners') sugar, for dusting

1 Preheat the oven to 180°C (350°F/Gas 4). Spray a 20 x 30 cm (8 x 12 inch) shallow baking tin with oil and line the base with baking paper.

2 Sift the flours, bicarbonate of soda and cocoa powder into a large bowl. Mix the eggs, sugar, vanilla essence, oil, fromage frais and purée in a separate large bowl, stirring until well combined. Add to the flour and stir until combined. Spread into the prepared tin and bake for about 30 minutes, or until a skewer inserted in the centre comes out clean.

3 The brownie will sink slightly in the centre as it cools. Leave in the tin for 5 minutes before turning onto a wire rack to cool. Dust with icing sugar before cutting into pieces to serve.

Stir together the eggs, sugar, vanilla essence, oil, fromage frais and apple purée.

Add the egg mixture to the flour and stir thoroughly until combined.

NUTRITION PER PIECE
Protein 2.5 g; Fat 3.5 g; Carbohydrate 2.5 g; Dietary Fibre 5 g; Cholesterol 20 mg; 595 kJ (140 Cal)

Rhubarb and pear crumble

PREPARATION TIME: 20 MINUTES | TOTAL COOKING TIME: 35 MINUTES | SERVES 6

600 g (1 lb 5 oz) rhubarb
2 strips lemon zest
1 tablespoon honey, or to taste
2 firm, ripe pears
50 g (1¾ oz/½ cup) rolled oats
35 g (1¼ oz/¼ cup) wholemeal (whole-wheat) plain (all-purpose) flour
60 g (2¼ oz/⅓ cup) soft brown sugar
50 g (1¾ oz) butter

1 Trim the rhubarb, wash and cut into 3 cm (1¼ inch) pieces. Place in a medium saucepan with the lemon zest and 1 tablespoon water. Cook, covered, over low heat for 10 minutes, or until tender. Cool a little. Stir in the honey and remove the lemon zest.

2 Preheat the oven to 180°C (350°F/Gas 4). Peel, core and cut the pears into 2 cm (¾ inch) cubes and combine with the rhubarb. Pour into a 1.25 litre (44 fl oz/5 cup) dish and smooth the surface.

3 To make the topping, combine the oats, flour and brown sugar in a bowl. Rub in the butter with your fingertips until the mixture is crumbly. Spread over the fruit. Bake for 15 minutes, or until cooked and golden.

NUTRITION PER SERVE
Protein 3.5 g; Fat 8 g; Carbohydrate 30 g; Dietary Fibre 6 g; Cholesterol 0 mg; 885 kJ (210 Cal)

Trim the rhubarb, wash thoroughly, then cut into short pieces.

Add the cubed pears to the cooked rhubarb and gently stir to combine.

Use your fingertips to rub the butter into the dry ingredients to make a crumble topping.

Pears poached in dark grape juice

PREPARATION TIME: 15 MINUTES + OVERNIGHT REFRIGERATION | TOTAL COOKING TIME: 1 HOUR 20 MINUTES | SERVES 6

6 beurre bosc (or any firm) pears
2 tablespoons lemon juice
500 ml (17 fl oz/2 cups) dark grape juice
500 ml (17 fl oz/2 cups) blackcurrant juice
2 tablespoons sweet sherry
4 cloves
350 g (12 oz) black grapes
250 g (9 oz/1 cup) low-fat plain yoghurt
½ teaspoon ground cinnamon
1 tablespoon honey

NUTRITION PER SERVE
Protein 4 g; Fat 0 g; Carbohydrate 95 g; Dietary Fibre 4 g; Cholesterol 2 mg; 1630 kJ (390 Cal)

1 Core and peel the pears, leaving the stalks on. Place the pears, as you peel, in a bowl filled with cold water and the lemon juice, to prevent browning.

2 Put the grape and blackcurrant juices, sherry and cloves in a saucepan large enough to hold the pears. Add the pears.

3 Bring the liquid to the boil, then reduce to a simmer. Cover and cook for 35–40 minutes, or until tender. Remove from the heat and leave the pears to cool in the syrup. Transfer the pears and syrup to a bowl and cover with plastic wrap. Refrigerate overnight.

4 To serve, strain the syrup into a saucepan, bring to the boil, then reduce to a simmer and cook for 40 minutes, or until reduced by about two-thirds. Cool slightly, place a pear on each plate and pour syrup over the pears. Arrange the grapes next to the pears. Just before serving, mix the yoghurt, cinnamon and honey and spoon over the pears or serve on the side.

Remove the core from the pears, then peel, leaving the stalks on.

Bring the liquid to the boil, then reduce the heat and simmer until tender.

Mix the yoghurt, cinnamon and honey just before serving the pears.

Banana and blueberry tart

PREPARATION TIME: 30 MINUTES | TOTAL COOKING TIME: 25 MINUTES | SERVES 6

125 g (4½ oz/1 cup) plain (all-purpose) flour
60 g (2¼ oz/½ cup) self-raising flour
1 teaspoon cinnamon
1 teaspoon ground ginger
40 g (1½ oz) butter, chopped
95 g (3¼ oz/½ cup) soft brown sugar
125 ml (4 fl oz/½ cup) buttermilk
200 g (7 oz) blueberries
2 ripe bananas
2 teaspoons lemon juice
1 tablespoon demerara sugar

1 Preheat the oven to 200°C (400°F/Gas 6). Lightly spray a baking tray or pizza tray with oil. Sift the flours and spices into a bowl. Add the butter and sugar and rub in until the mixture resembles breadcrumbs. Make a well and then add enough buttermilk to mix to a soft dough.

2 Roll the dough out on a lightly floured surface to a 23 cm (9 inch) diameter round. Place on the tray and roll the edge to form a rim.

3 Spread the blueberries over the dough, keeping within the rim. Slice the bananas, toss them in the lemon juice, then arrange over the top. Sprinkle with the sugar and bake for 25 minutes, until the base is browned. Serve immediately.

Rub the butter into the flour until the mixture resembles breadcrumbs.

Put the circle of dough on the tray and roll the edge to form a rim.

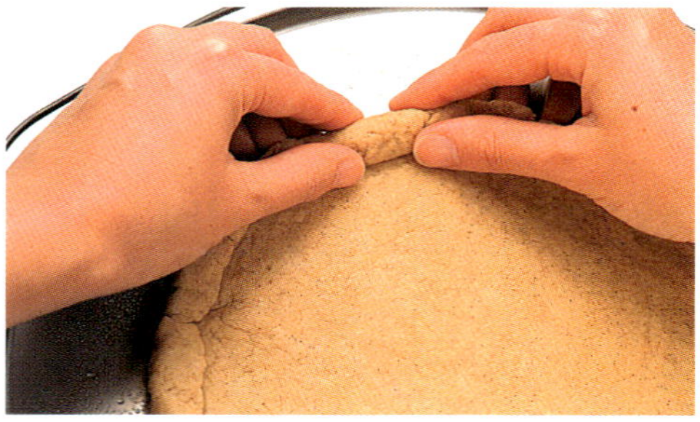

NUTRITION PER SERVE
Protein 5 g; Fat 6 g; Carbohydrate 55 g; Dietary Fibre 3 g; Cholesterol 20 mg; 1215 kJ (290 Cal)

Carrot cake

PREPARATION TIME: 20 MINUTES | TOTAL COOKING TIME: 1 HOUR 15 MINUTES | MAKES 14 SLICES

310 g (11 oz/2½ cups) self-raising flour
1 teaspoon bicarbonate of soda (baking soda)
2 teaspoons ground cinnamon
1 teaspoon mixed (pumpkin pie) spice
95 g (3¼ oz/½ cup) soft brown sugar
60 g (2¼ oz/½ cup) sultanas (golden raisins)
2 eggs, lightly beaten
2 tablespoons vegetable oil
4 tablespoons low-fat milk
140 g (5 oz) apple purée
300 g (10½ oz) carrot, coarsely grated

RICOTTA TOPPING

125 g (4½ oz/½ cup) ricotta cheese
30 g (1 oz/¼ cup) icing (confectioners') sugar
½ teaspoon grated lime zest

1 Grease a 10 x 18 cm (4 x 7 inch) loaf tin and line the base with baking paper. Preheat the oven to 180°C (350°F/Gas 4). Sift the flour, bicarbonate of soda and spices into a large bowl. Stir in the sugar and sultanas.

2 Mix the eggs, oil, milk and apple purée and stir into the dry ingredients. Stir in the carrot. Spread into the tin and bake for 1¼ hours, or until a skewer comes out clean. Cool in the tin for 5 minutes, then cool completely on a wire rack.

3 To make the topping, beat the ingredients together until smooth. Spread over the cake.

Stir the egg and apple mixture into the dry ingredients, then stir in the carrot.

A skewer inserted into the centre of the cake should come out clean when it is cooked.

NUTRITION PER SLICE
Protein 4.5 g; Fat 5 g; Carbohydrate 30 g; Dietary Fibre 2 g; Cholesterol 30 mg; 755 kJ (180 Cal)

Passionfruit tart

PREPARATION TIME: 25 MINUTES + 30 MINUTES REFRIGERATION | TOTAL COOKING TIME: 1 HOUR | SERVES 8

90 g (3¼ oz/¾ cup) plain (all-purpose) flour
2 tablespoons icing (confectioners') sugar
2 tablespoons custard powder
30 g (1 oz) butter
3 tablespoons light evaporated milk

FILLING
125 g (4½ oz/½ cup) ricotta cheese
1 teaspoon vanilla essence
30 g (1 oz/¼ cup) icing (confectioners') sugar, plus extra, for dusting
2 eggs, lightly beaten
4 tablespoons passionfruit pulp (about 8 passionfruit)
185 ml (6 fl oz/¾ cup) light evaporated milk

NUTRITION PER SERVE
Protein 8 g; Fat 6.5 g; Carbohydrate 25 g; Dietary Fibre 3 g; Cholesterol 65 mg; 750 kJ (180 Cal)

1 Preheat the oven to 200°C (400°F/Gas 6). Lightly spray a 23 cm (9 inch) loose-based flan (tart) tin with oil. Sift the flour, icing sugar and custard powder into a bowl and rub in the butter until crumbs form. Add enough evaporated milk to form a soft dough. Bring together on a floured surface until just smooth. Gather into a ball, wrap in plastic and chill for 15 minutes.

2 Roll the pastry out on a floured surface to fit the tin, then refrigerate for a further 15 minutes. Cover with baking paper and fill with rice or dried beans. Bake for 10 minutes, remove the rice or beans and paper and bake for another 5–8 minutes, or until golden. Allow to cool. Reduce the oven to 160°C (315°F/Gas 2–3).

3 Beat the ricotta with the vanilla essence and icing sugar until smooth. Add the eggs, passionfruit pulp and evaporated milk, then beat well. Put the tin with the pastry case on a baking tray and pour in the filling. Bake for 40 minutes, or until set. Cool in the tin. Dust with icing sugar to serve, if desired.

Remove the baking paper and rice or beans and blind bake the pastry case again.

When the ricotta mixture is smooth, add the eggs, passionfruit pulp and milk.

Put the tin on a baking tray to catch any drips and gently pour in the filling.

Oat and date muffins

PREPARATION TIME: 20 MINUTES | TOTAL COOKING TIME: 18 MINUTES | MAKES 12

125 g (4½ oz/1 cup) self-raising flour
150 g (5½ oz/1 cup) wholemeal (whole-wheat) self-raising flour
½ teaspoon bicarbonate of soda (baking soda)
100 g (3½ oz/1 cup) quick rolled oats
55 g (1¾ oz/¼ cup) soft brown sugar
185 g (6½ oz) chopped dates
1 egg
2 tablespoons vegetable oil
90 g (3¼ oz/¼ cup) golden syrup
310 ml (10¾ fl oz/1¼ cups) skim milk
cooking oil spray

1 Sift the self-raising and wholemeal self-raising flours with the bicarbonate of soda into a large bowl. Return the husks to the bowl.

2 Stir in the quick rolled oats, brown sugar and chopped dates. Make a well in the centre.

3 Beat together the egg, oil, syrup and skim milk in a bowl. Pour into the dry ingredients and stir with a large metal spoon until just combined. The mixture will look lumpy. Do not overmix.

4 Preheat the oven to 200°C (400°F/Gas 6). Lightly spray a 12-hole muffin tin with oil. (The holes should have a 125 ml (4 fl oz/½ cup) capacity.) Spoon the mixture into the tin. Bake for 18 minutes, or until well risen and golden. Leave in the tin for 5 minutes before turning onto a wire rack to cool.

When you have sifted the flours, return the husks to the bowl.

Stir the mixture with a large metal spoon, until just combined.

NUTRITION PER MUFFIN
Protein 5 g; Fat 5 g; Carbohydrate 15 g; Dietary Fibre 4 g; Cholesterol 15 mg; 910 kJ (220 Cal)

Fruit jellies

PREPARATION TIME: 20 MINUTES + REFRIGERATION | TOTAL COOKING TIME: NIL | SERVES 4

4 teaspoons gelatine
500 ml (17 fl oz/2 cups) cranberry and raspberry juice
325 g (11½ oz) mixed berries, fresh or frozen

1 Sprinkle the gelatine in an even layer onto 3 tablespoons of the juice, in a small bowl, and leave to go spongy. Bring a small saucepan of water to the boil, remove from the heat and place the bowl in the pan. The water should come halfway up the side of the bowl. Stir the gelatine until clear and dissolved. Cool slightly and mix with the rest of the juice.

2 Rinse four 185 ml (6 fl oz/¾ cup) moulds with water (wet moulds make it easier when unmoulding) and pour 2 cm (¾ inch) of the juice into each. Refrigerate until set. Meanwhile, if the fruit is frozen, defrost it and add any liquid to the remaining juice. When the bottom layer of jelly has set, divide the fruit among the moulds (reserving a few berries to garnish) and divide the rest of the juice among the moulds, pouring it over the fruit. Refrigerate until set.

3 To turn out the jellies, hold each mould in a hot, damp tea towel (dish towel) and turn out onto a plate. Ease away the edge of the jelly with your finger to break the seal. (If you turn the jellies onto a damp plate you will be able to move them around, otherwise they will stick.) Garnish with reserved berries.

Lower the gelatine bowl into the hot water and stir the gelatine until dissolved.

Use your finger to ease away the edge of the jelly and break the seal.

NUTRITION PER SERVE
Protein 3 g; Fat 0 g; Carbohydrate 25 g; Dietary Fibre 1.5 g; Cholesterol 0 mg; 420 kJ (100 Cal)

Meringue baskets with fruit

PREPARATION TIME: 40 MINUTES + COOLING | TOTAL COOKING TIME: 1 HOUR 30 MINUTES | SERVES 6

2 egg whites
small pinch cream of tartar
125 g (4½ oz/½ cup) caster (superfine) sugar
2 tablespoons custard powder
500 ml (17 fl oz/2 cups) skim milk
1 teaspoon vanilla essence
1 peach, cut into thin wedges
1 kiwi fruit, cut into thin wedges
6 strawberries, cut in half
2 tablespoons apricot jam

NUTRITION PER SERVE
Protein 5 g; Fat 0.5 g; Carbohydrate 30 g; Dietary Fibre 1 g; Cholesterol 3 mg; 590 kJ (140 Cal)

1 Preheat the oven to low 150°C (300°F/ Gas 2) and line a baking tray with baking paper. Beat the egg whites and cream of tartar with electric beaters until soft peaks form. Gradually add the sugar and beat until it is dissolved and the mixture is stiff and glossy.

2 Fit a piping bag with a medium star nozzle and pipe coiled spirals of the meringue (about 7½ cm/3 inches) onto the tray. Pipe an extra ring around the top edge to make baskets. Bake for 30 minutes, then reduce the heat to 120°C (235°F/Gas ½). Bake for 45 minutes, turn the oven off and cool with the oven door ajar.

3 Mix the custard powder with a little of the milk to form a smooth paste. Transfer to a saucepan with the remaining milk and the vanilla essence. Stir over medium heat until the mixture boils and thickens. Remove from the heat and place plastic wrap over the surface to stop a skin forming. Set aside and, when cool, stir until smooth. Spoon some of the cold custard into each basket. Top with fruit. Heat the jam until liquid, then brush over the fruit to glaze.

Beat the egg whites and cream of tartar until soft peaks form.

Pipe an extra ring around the top edge of the coils to make baskets.

Lay a piece of plastic wrap directly onto the surface of the custard.

Blueberry and almond muffins

PREPARATION TIME: 15 MINUTES | TOTAL COOKING TIME: 18 MINUTES | MAKES 12

250 g (9 oz/2 cups) self-raising flour
60 g (2 oz/¼ cup) caster (superfine) sugar
250 ml (9 fl oz/1 cup) skim milk
1 egg, lightly beaten
1 teaspoon vanilla essence
2 tablespoons melted butter
200 g (7 oz) blueberries
1 tablespoon demerara sugar
30 g (1 oz) chopped almonds

1 Sift the flour into a large bowl. Stir in the caster sugar and make a well in the centre.

2 In a bowl, combine the skim milk, egg, vanilla essence and melted butter. Pour into the dry ingredients and stir with a large metal spoon until just combined. The mixture will look lumpy. Do not overmix. Quickly stir through the blueberries.

3 Preheat the oven to 200°C (400°F/Gas 6). Lightly spray a 12-hole muffin tin with oil. (The holes should have a 125 ml (4 fl oz/½ cup) capacity.) Spoon the mixture into the tin and sprinkle with the sugar combined with chopped almonds. Bake for 18 minutes, or until golden. Leave in the tin for 5 minutes before turning onto a wire rack to cool.

NUTRITION PER MUFFIN
Protein 3.5 g; Fat 3 g; Carbohydrate 25 g; Dietary Fibre 1 g; Cholesterol 15 mg; 595 kJ (145 Cal)

Spoon the mixture into the tin and sprinkle with sugar combined with almonds.

Raspberry mousse

PREPARATION TIME: 30 MINUTES + REFRIGERATION | TOTAL COOKING TIME: NIL | SERVES 4

3 teaspoons gelatine
250 g (9 oz/1 cup) low-fat vanilla yoghurt
2 x 200 g (7 oz) tubs low-fat fromage frais or light vanilla Fruche
4 egg whites
150 g (5½ oz) raspberries, mashed
extra raspberries and mint leaves, for serving

1 Sprinkle the gelatine in an even layer onto 1 tablespoon water in a small bowl and leave to go spongy. Bring a small saucepan of water to the boil, remove from the heat and place the bowl in the pan. Stir until clear.

2 In a large bowl, stir the vanilla yoghurt and fromage frais together, then add the gelatine and mix well.

3 Using electric beaters, beat the egg whites until stiff peaks form, then fold through the yoghurt mixture. Transfer half to a separate bowl and fold the mashed raspberries through.

4 Divide the raspberry mixture into the bases of four long glasses or serving bowls. Top with the vanilla mixture. Refrigerate for several hours, or until set. Decorate with fresh raspberries and mint leaves.

NUTRITION PER SERVE
Protein 9.5 g; Fat 2 g; Carbohydrate 10 g; Dietary Fibre 2 g; Cholesterol 4 mg; 355 kJ (85 Cal)

You can use fresh raspberries or frozen. Thaw frozen raspberries completely before mashing.

Stir the yoghurt and fromage frais together until combined.

Gently fold the mashed raspberries through half the yoghurt mixture.

Fruit tarts

PREPARATION TIME: 25 MINUTES + 30 MINUTES REFRIGERATION | TOTAL COOKING TIME: 20 MINUTES | MAKES 8

125 g (4½ oz/1 cup) plain (all-purpose) flour
30 g (1 oz/¼ cup) custard powder
30 g (1 oz/¼ cup) icing (confectioners') sugar
40 g (1½ oz) butter
2 tablespoons low-fat milk
2 x 130 g (4½ oz) tubs low-fat strawberry fromage frais or light strawberry Fruche
100 g (3½ oz) ricotta cheese
halved strawberries, blueberries, kiwi fruit, peeled and sliced
2 tablespoons apricot jam

NUTRITION PER TART
Protein 3.5 g; Fat 8 g; Carbohydrate 20 g; Dietary Fibre 1 g; Cholesterol 20 mg; 690 kJ (165 Cal)

1 Grease eight 7 cm (2¾ inch) loose-based flan (tart) tins. Mix the flour, custard powder, icing sugar and butter in a food processor until fine crumbs form, then add enough of the milk to form a soft dough. Gather into a ball, wrap in plastic and chill for 30 minutes.

2 Preheat the oven to 200°C (400°F/Gas 6). Divide the dough into eight portions and roll out to line the tins. Cover with paper and rice or dried beans. Bake for 10 minutes, remove the paper and rice and bake for another 10 minutes, or until golden. Cool and remove from the tins.

3 Mix the fromage frais and ricotta until smooth. Spread over the pastry bases and top with assorted fruit. Heat the jam until liquid, then brush over the fruit to glaze.

Add enough milk to the crumbly mixture to form a soft dough.

To blind bake, cover the pastry with baking paper and fill with uncooked rice or beans.

Remove the rice or beans and paper and return the pastry to the oven until golden.

Strawberry and banana ice

PREPARATION TIME: 10 MINUTES + FREEZING | TOTAL COOKING TIME: NIL | SERVES 4

300 g (10½ oz) silken tofu, chopped
250 g (9 oz) strawberries, chopped
2 ripe bananas, chopped
60 g (2¼ oz/¼ cup) caster (superfine) sugar

1 Blend the silken tofu, strawberries, banana and caster sugar in a blender or food processor, until smooth.

2 Pour the mixture into a shallow cake tin and freeze until almost frozen. Remove from the freezer and break up roughly with a fork or a spoon, then transfer to a large bowl and beat until it has a smooth texture. Pour the mixture evenly into a 15 x 25 cm (6 x 10 inch) loaf tin, cover and freeze again, until quite firm.

3 Alternatively, freeze the blended mixture in an ice cream machine until thick and creamy, then store in a covered container in the freezer.

4 Transfer to the refrigerator for about 30 minutes before serving to allow the ice to soften slightly.

NUTRITION PER SERVE
Protein 7 g; Fat 3 g; Carbohydrate 30 g; Dietary Fibre 3 g; Cholesterol 0 mg; 710 kJ (170 Cal)

Blend the tofu, strawberries, banana and caster sugar until smooth.

When partially frozen, use a fork or spoon to break up the mixture.

Transfer the chopped mixture to a bowl and beat until smooth.

Raisin, banana and apple muffins

PREPARATION TIME: 20 MINUTES | TOTAL COOKING TIME: 20 MINUTES | MAKES 12

200 g (7 oz/1¼ cups) chopped raisins
125 g (4½ oz/1 cup) self-raising flour
150 g (5½ oz/1 cup) wholemeal (whole-wheat) self-raising flour
1 teaspoon ground cinnamon
95 g (3¼ oz/½ cup) soft brown sugar
135 g (4¾ oz/½ cup) apple sauce
1 egg
250 ml (9 fl oz/1 cup) skim milk
2 tablespoons vegetable oil
1 ripe banana, mashed
cooking oil spray
2 tablespoons rolled oats
1 tablespoon soft brown sugar, extra

1 Place the raisins in a bowl, cover with boiling water, set aside for 30 minutes, then drain.

2 Sift the self-raising and wholemeal self-raising flours, cinnamon and soft brown sugar into a large bowl.

3 Mix the apple sauce, egg and skim milk in a bowl. Stir in the oil and mashed banana. Stir the apple mixture and raisins into the flour with a large metal spoon until just combined. The mixture will look lumpy. Do not overmix.

4 Preheat the oven to 200°C (400°F/Gas 6). Lightly spray a 12-hole muffin tin with oil. (The holes should have a 125 ml (4 fl oz/½ cup) capacity.) Spoon the mixture into the tin and sprinkle with the rolled oats combined with the sugar. Bake for 20 minutes, or until cooked through. Leave in the tin for 5 minutes before turning onto a wire rack to cool.

Stir the vegetable oil and mashed banana into the mixture.

Spoon the mixture into the tin and sprinkle with the rolled oats.

NUTRITION PER MUFFIN
Protein 4.5 g; Fat 4 g; Carbohydrate 40 g; Dietary Fibre 3 g; Cholesterol 15 mg; 880 kJ (210 Cal)

Basics—dressings

Dressings

Herb, garlic and yoghurt

MAKES 250 ML (9 FL OZ/1 CUP)

Whisk together 200 g (7 oz) low-fat plain yoghurt, 4 tablespoons skim milk, 1 teaspoon dijon mustard, 1 tablespoon finely snipped chives, 2 teaspoons finely chopped parsley, 2 teaspoons chopped oregano and 1 crushed garlic clove. Season with salt and pepper.

NUTRITION PER TABLESPOON
Protein 1 g; Fat 0 g; Carbohydrate 1 g; Dietary Fibre 0 g; Cholesterol 0 mg; 50 kJ (10 Cal)

Berry dressing

MAKES 185 ML (6 FL OZ/¾ CUP)

Blend 100 g (3½ oz) fresh or thawed frozen strawberries, 1½ tablespoons oil, 3 tablespoons apple juice, 1 tablespoon lemon juice, 1 tablespoon cider vinegar and some cracked black pepper in a blender until smooth. Season with salt.

NUTRITION PER TABLESPOON
Protein 0 g; Fat 3 g; Carbohydrate 1 g; Dietary Fibre 0 g; Cholesterol 0 mg; 145 kJ (35 Cal)

Walnut vinaigrette

MAKES 125 ML (4 FL OZ/½ CUP)

Combine 2 tablespoons cider vinegar, 1 tablespoon balsamic vinegar, 1½ tablespoons walnut oil, 1 teaspoon dijon mustard, 2 tablespoons water, ½ teaspoon caster (superfine) sugar and 2 teaspoons finely chopped parsley in a screw top jar. Shake the jar, then season.

NUTRITION PER TABLESPOON
Protein 0 g; Fat 5 g; Carbohydrate 1 g; Dietary Fibre 0 g; Cholesterol 0 mg; 210 kJ (50 Cal)

Roasted capsicum sauce

MAKES 250 ML (9 FL OZ/1 CUP)

Quarter two red capsicums (peppers), remove the seeds and membrane and grill (broil) until the skins blister and blacken. Cool under a damp tea towel (dish towel) before peeling. Cut one quarter into thin strips then set aside. Heat 1 teaspoon oil in a small saucepan, add 2 finely chopped spring onions (scallions) and 1 tablespoon water, then stir over heat until the spring onion is soft. Add the remaining capsicum, 3 tablespoons beef stock, 2 tablespoons white wine, 2 tablespoons tomato paste (concentrated purée) and ¼ teaspoon sugar. Simmer for 2 minutes, then blend until smooth. Season and stir in 1 tablespoon of snipped chives. Garnish with reserved red capsicum strips.

NUTRITION PER TABLESPOON
Protein 0.5 g; Fat 0.5 g; Carbohydrate 1.5 g; Dietary Fibre 0.5 g; Cholesterol 0 mg; 55 kJ (15 Cal)

Tomato sauce

MAKES 500 ML (17 FL OZ/2 CUPS)

Heat 1 teaspoon oil in a saucepan, add a sliced small leek, 2 tablespoons water and 1 crushed garlic clove. Cover and stir until the leek is soft. Add a 440 g (15½ oz) tin chopped tomato, 1 tablespoon tomato paste (concentrated purée), ¼ teaspoon sugar and 2 tablespoons red wine. Stir, then simmer for 5 minutes. Season.

NUTRITION PER TABLESPOON
Protein 0.5 g; Fat 0.5 g; Carbohydrate 1.5 g; Dietary Fibre 0.5 g; Cholesterol 0 mg; 55 kJ (15 Cal)

Hummus dressing

MAKES 250 ML (9 FL OZ/1 CUP)

Drain a 425 g (15 oz) tin chickpeas and put in a food processor with 185 ml (6 fl oz/¾ cup) vegetable stock, 1 tablespoon tahini paste and 2 chopped garlic cloves. Stir 1 teaspoon each of ground coriander and cumin in a dry frying pan over medium heat for 3 minutes, or until aromatic. Cool slightly, add to the processor and mix until nearly smooth. Mix in 2 tablespoons lemon juice. Season with cracked pepper and salt. If too thick, add a little water.

NUTRITION PER TABLESPOON
Protein 2 g; Fat 1.5 g; Carbohydrate 4 g; Dietary Fibre 1.5 g; Cholesterol 0 mg; 160 kJ (40 Cal)

Sweet ricotta cream

MAKES 250 ML (9 FL OZ/1 CUP)

Beat together 200 g (7 oz) ricotta cheese, 100 g (3½ oz) low-fat plain yoghurt, ½ teaspoon finely grated orange zest, 3 tablespoons orange juice and 1 tablespoon caster (superfine) sugar until smooth.

NUTRITION PER TABLESPOON
Protein 2 g; Fat 1.5 g; Carbohydrate 2.5 g; Dietary Fibre 0 g; Cholesterol 6.5 mg; 130 kJ (30 Cal)

The low-down on low fat

Fat is often portrayed as a villain and we must remember that it is not—everyone needs a certain amount of fat in their body, to help with growth and development and to carry fat-soluble vitamins throughout the body. It is the quantity and type of fat we eat that can cause problems. Foods contain a mix of different fats, but one type usually predominates in each food.

Saturated fats, those that have been implicated in some health problems and can raise cholesterol levels, are found mainly in animal products, including butter, cream, fat on meat and other fats which are solid at room temperature, like dripping or lard. Monounsaturated fats, which are generally regarded as being better for us, are found in olives, olive oil, many vegetable oils, most nuts, avocados and, in small amounts, in fish, chicken, lean meat and also eggs.

Polyunsaturated fats, found in nuts, grains, seeds and oily fish, usually remain soft at room temperature and also do not have the poor health implications of saturated fats. However, although some fats are undoubtedly better for us than others, most tend to be high in kilojoules. So if you are wanting to reduce the fat in your diet, don't eat too many nuts or avocados. If you are aiming to lose weight, cutting back on your fat intake is a good place to start and this book will certainly help you monitor that, but you do also need to consult your doctor and take advice about an exercise program.

If you want to limit your fat intake, it is recommended you have no more than about 30–40 g of fat per day (30 g for women and small men, 40 g for men and taller women). With this in mind, we have developed recipes with the following amounts of fat per serve:

- soups and starters with up to 8 g fat
- main courses with up to 15 g fat
- desserts with up to 8 g fat.

You will find a variety of recipes, from hearty family dinners to dishes suitable for entertaining. Eating low-fat doesn't mean missing out on anything.

Helpful ingredients

As well as using the recipes in this book, once you get used to cooking and eating the low-fat way, you will find you don't need to completely give up many of your favourite dishes but you can adapt them yourself by using lower-fat ingredients. There are simple ways to change your cooking habits and other ways will become obvious when you use the recipes. Try low-fat natural yoghurt instead of sour cream, or whipped ricotta cheese with orange instead of whipped cream. Use fish canned in brine or spring water instead of oil. Buy chicken breast fillets that are sold without the skin, or remove the skin when you unpack them.

These days we are lucky with the choice and variety of low-fat foods available—dairy products such as cheese and spreads for bread, and meat which is sold well trimmed and labelled according to its fat content. The lean pre-trimmed cuts of meat (pork and lamb as well as beef) are excellent for making your own minced meat. Some shop-bought minced meat has quite a high proportion of fat, so make your own in a food processor. Avoid sausages, pies, pasties and burgers as these are made from poorer quality meat with higher proportions of fat. Eat more seafood, chicken and turkey (with the skin removed).

For those who love cheese, there are many fat-reduced cheddar cheeses on the market but it is also worth knowing that other cheeses, such as feta and ricotta, have low-fat versions.

Read all the labels on food packaging. These will tell you how much fat is contained in a recommended serving size or in a 100 g (3½ oz) portion. If there isn't a nutritional table on the packaging, the manufacturers must list the ingredients in order of the quantities used. If the fat is near the top of the list, try another brand.

Be aware that just because a product is labelled 'light', this doesn't necessarily mean light in fat: it can mean low in salt, flavour, colour and weight or low in alcohol. Also, don't be confused by foods claiming to be low-cholesterol or no-cholesterol—this doesn't necessarily mean low in fat—just low in animal fats. These foods, which may include nuts, nut products, margarines or oils, can still contain a high percentage of other fats. Processed foods tend to be higher in fat. The more natural and less prepared the food, the better it is for you.

Index

Index

Published by Bay Books, an imprint of Murdoch Books Pty Limited.

Murdoch Books Australia
Pier 8/9, 23 Hickson Road
Millers Point NSW 2000
Phone: + 61 (0) 2 8220 2000
Fax: + 61 (0) 2 8220 2558
www.murdochbooks.com.au

Chief Executive: Juliet Rogers
Publishing Director: Kay Scarlett

Project manager and editor: Paul O'Beirne
Design concept: Heather Menzies
Design: Heather Menzies and Jacqueline Richards
Photographer: Alan Benson
Stylist: Mary Harris
Food preparation: Joanne Glynn, Samantha Joel and Claire Pietersen
Introduction text: Leanne Kitchen
Production: Nikla Martin

ISBN 978 0 681 53382 0

Printed by i-Book Printing Ltd. PRINTED IN CHINA.
This edition published 2008.

IMPORTANT: Those who might be at risk from the effects of salmonella poisoning (the elderly, pregnant women, young children and those suffering from immune deficiency diseases) should consult their doctor with any concerns about eating raw eggs.

CONVERSION GUIDE: You may find cooking times vary depending on the oven you are using. For fan-forced ovens, as a general rule, set the oven temperature to 20°C (35°F) lower than indicated in the recipe.

NUTRITION: The nutritional information given for each recipe does not include any accompaniments, such as rice or pasta, unless they are included in the ingredients list. The nutritional values are approximations and can be affected by biological and seasonal variations in foods, the unknown composition of some manufactured foods and uncertainty in the dietary database. Nutrient data given are derived primarily from the official NUTTAB95 database.